Typical and Atypical Child and Adolescent Development 1

Theory and Methodology

This concise guide offers an accessible introduction to the key theoretical perspectives and methodologies in developmental psychology. It integrates insights from typical and atypical development to reveal fundamental aspects of human growth and development, and common developmental disorders.

The topic books in this series draw on international research in the field and are informed by biological, social and cultural perspectives, offering explanations of developmental phenomena with a focus on how children and adolescents at different ages actually think, feel and act. In this succinct volume, Stephen von Tetzchner outlines the main theoretical perspectives including psychodynamic psychology, behaviorism, logical constructivism, social constructivism, evolutionary psychology, ethological psychology, ecological psychology, information processing and critical developmental psychology. He provides a guide to methods of gaining knowledge about children and introduces child and adolescent disorders.

Together with a companion website that offers topic-based quizzes, lecturer PowerPoint slides and sample essay questions, *Typical and Atypical Child and Adolescent Development 1: Theory and Methodology* is an essential text for all students of developmental psychology, as well as those working in the fields of child development, developmental disabilities and special education.

Stephen von Tetzchner is Professor of Developmental Psychology at the Department of Psychology, University of Oslo, Norway.

The content of this topic book is taken from Stephen von Tetzchner's core textbook *Child and Adolescent Psychology: Typical and Atypical Development*. The comprehensive volume offers a complete overview of child and adolescent development. For more information, visit www.routledge.com/9781138823396

Topics from Child and Adolescent Psychology Series
Stephen von Tetzchner

The **Topics from Child and Adolescent Psychology Series** offers concise guides on key aspects of child and adolescent development. They are formed from selected chapters from Stephen von Tetzchner's comprehensive textbook *Child and Adolescent Psychology: Typical and Atypical Development* and are intended to be accessible introductions for students of relevant modules on developmental psychology courses, as well as for professionals working in the fields of child development, developmental disabilities and special education. The topic books explain the key aspects of human development by integrating insights from typical and atypical development to cement understanding of the processes involved and the work with children who have developmental disorders. They examine sensory, physical and cognitive disabilities and the main emotional and behavioral disorders of childhood and adolescence, as well as the developmental consequences of these disabilities and disorders.

Topics books in the series

Typical and Atypical Child and Adolescent Development 1
Theoretical Perspectives and Methodology

Typical and Atypical Child and Adolescent Development 2
Genes, Fetal Development and Early Neurological Development

Typical and Atypical Child and Adolescent Development 3
Perceptual and Motor Development

Typical and Atypical Child and Adolescent Development 4
Cognition, Intelligence and Learning

Typical and Atypical Child and Adolescent Development 5
Communication and Language Development

Typical and Atypical Child and Adolescent Development 6
Emotions, Temperament, Personality, Moral, Prosocial and Antisocial Development

Typical and Atypical Child and Adolescent Development 7
Social Relations, Self-awareness and Identity

For more information on individual topic books visit www.routledge.com/Topics-from-Child-and-Adolescent-Psychology/book-series/TFCAAP

Typical and Atypical Child and Adolescent Development 1

Theory and Methodology

Stephen von Tetzchner

Routledge
Taylor & Francis Group

LONDON AND NEW YORK

Cover image: John M Lund Photography Inc

First published 2023
by Routledge
4 Park Square, Milton Park, Abingdon, Oxon OX14 4RN

and by Routledge
605 Third Avenue, New York, NY 10158

Routledge is an imprint of the Taylor & Francis Group, an informa business

British Library Cataloguing-in-Publication Data
A catalogue record for this book is available from the British Library

Library of Congress Cataloging-in-Publication Data
A catalog record has been requested for this book

ISBN: 978-1-032-27085-2 (hbk)
ISBN: 978-1-032-26760-9 (pbk)
ISBN: 978-1-003-29127-5 (ebk)

DOI: 10.4324/9781003291275

Typeset in Bembo
by Apex CoVantage, LLC

Access the companion website: www.routledge.com/cw/vonTetzchner

Contents

Introduction   x

PART I
Developmental Psychology   1

1   Psychology and Development   3

2   The Historical Roots of Developmental Psychology   5

3   Globalization   7

4   Typical and Atypical Development   9

5   Recurrent Issues in Developmental Psychology   11

6   Modeling Development   15

7   Dynamic Systems   23

8   Vulnerability, Risk, Resilience and Protection   28

9   The Developmental Way of Thinking   32

    Summary of Part I   35

    Core Issues   36

    Suggestions for Further Reading   36

PART II
Theoretical Perspectives   **37**

10 The Function of Developmental Theories   39
11 Psychodynamic Psychology   42
12 Behaviorism   47
13 Logical Constructivism   52
14 Social Constructivism   56
15 Evolutionary Psychology   60
16 Ethological Psychology   63
17 Ecological Psychology   64
18 Information Processing   68
19 Critical Developmental Psychology   70
20 Distinguishing between Theories   72
     Summary of Part II   75
     Core Issues   77
     Suggestions for Further Reading   77

PART III
Methods of Gaining Knowledge about Children   **79**

21 Observations   81
22 Questionnaires and Interviews   86
23 Archival Research   88
24 Methodologies   89
25 Special Methods for Studying Infants   96
26 Criteria for Research Methodology   100

27   Assessment   104

28   Ethical Considerations   111

     Summary of Part III   112

     Core Issues   114

     Suggestions for Further Reading   114

PART IV
Child and Adolescent Disorders   **115**

29   Categorization of Disorders and Classification Systems   117

30   Sensory Impairments   120

31   Motor Impairments   123

32   Neurodevelopmental Disorders   125

33   Behavioral and Emotional Disorders   133

34   Trauma and Stressor-Related Disorders   141

35   Addictions   144

36   Acquired Disorders   146

     Summary of Part IV   147

     Core Issues   149

     Suggestions for Further Reading   149

     Glossary   151
     Bibliography   169
     Index   197

Introduction

This volume represents four pillars in the study of child **development** and the developmental way of thinking: **Concepts**, theories, methods and categorization of **developmental disorders**. They constitute basic tools for understanding typical and **atypical development** in general and within the various developmental **domains** presented in the other topic books (and the complete textbook).

Part I Developmental Psychology presents basic concepts and models, recurrent or core issues, and applications of the developmental way of thinking. Concepts are needed for describing children's abilities and how they function in various domains, while models are used for explaining how different factors influence development. Many of the concepts may be found in the Glossary. This part emphasizes the historical roots of developmental psychology and the present trend towards greater cultural variety and globalization in developmental scientific thinking.

The core issues are discussed in most of the volumes. They include nature and nurture, that is, how influences from genes and environment interact in development, and the question of **continuity** or **discontinuity** in abilities and skills through development. The presence of sensitive or **critical periods** in development, for example the ease of learning language in the early compared with later years, is important both for understanding the significance of the child's experiences in different phases of development and as a theoretical basis for early **childhood** intervention. Observing a child's developmental achievements and challenges in different phases of development is important, but, in the developmental way of thinking, attention is given rather to the underlying processes that may promote or hinder mental growth. Only if these processes are understood may it be possible to reduce the **risk** of negative developmental outcomes.

Development from the **germinal period** to adulthood involves complex processes and, hence, requires complex explanatory models. There is rarely a direct one-to-one relation between a biological or environmental factor and a developmental outcome (**main effect**). It is **interaction effects** that characterize child and adolescent development, meaning that the effect of one factor on development usually is moderated by one or several other factors. For example, children's early **temperament** may influence how they react to the newness or stress and cope in various situations. The early models of child development assumed that the influence was one-sided, that the child's development was influenced by positive and negative features of the environment. However, in the 1970s, researchers became aware of how children also influence their environment. In modern developmental psychology, development is perceived as a *transactional process*, with mutual influences between the child and the environment over time.

Important for the application of the developmental way of thinking is the *dynamic systems model*, where imbalances in functioning lead to developmental change and the emergence of new skills and abilities. Many children develop *vulnerabilities* or grow up in environments that represent *risks* for deviant development. On the other hand, there are environments that seem to protect vulnerable children and children who seem to be *resilient* to severe environmental risks. Small developmental obstacles sometimes develop into *cascades*, that is, sequences of problems which increase in scope and magnitude. This emphasizes that developmental risks may be cumulative. It is a general aim of developmental psychology to uncover the processes that may lead to positive or negative developmental outcomes. Central in clinical child psychology is **developmental psychopathology**, which seeks to reveal and influence the processes that can give rise to mental health problems in children and adolescents and uncover factors that can promote or inhibit the development of anxiety, depression and other psychological disorders.

Theories are intellectual tools for making sense of observations of children and adolescents, of their actions and reactions, social and mental functioning, early and later social relations, and how they adapt and cope in their environments. *Part II Theoretical Perspectives* presents the basic ideas and historical contexts of the main theoretical perspectives on child and adolescent development. Each of these perspectives constitutes its own universe of related ideas and assumptions, which may be closer or farther away from the ideas and assumptions of the other theoretical universes. There are many similarities across the perspectives, but they differ in their emphasis on developmental domains and their explanations of developmental phenomena. The mental psychological structures that are a core feature of **psychodynamic theories** are very different from the **attachment** process and mental **working models** described by ethological theory. Both address different aspects of development than **logical constructivism** with a focus on **cognitive structure**.

Comparisons of the theoretical perspectives give insights into the issues and challenges involved in explaining the physical, mental and social changes from **infancy** to adulthood and the factors that may govern these processes. Knowledge of one theory is never enough. A comprehensive understanding of child and adolescent development must rest on thorough knowledge of the different theories, their agreements and disagreements – sometimes fierce – about both descriptions and explanations of developmental phenomena.

More detailed elements of the theories related to specific domains are presented in the other topic books. For example, psychodynamic theories of personality are presented in Book 6, *Emotions, Temperament, Personality, Moral, Prosocial and Antisocial Development*, Piaget's logical constructivist theory on **perception** is presented in Book 3, *Perceptual and Motor Development*, and his cognitive theory in Book 4, *Cognition, Intelligence and Learning*.

Insights into child and adolescent development build on systematic knowledge of how children and adolescents at different ages think and how they act and react in different activities and contexts. *Part III Methods of Gaining Knowledge about Children* presents a wide range of methods for gathering information about children, including different forms of observations, **experiments**, interviews, **checklists** and **tests**. Qualitative and quantitative methodologies complement each other, and it is the research questions that decide which methods are best suited. **Quantitative methods** are used when there are behaviors, test scores, emotional expressions or other things that can be counted or measured, typically based on research questions starting with *who, where, when, what* or *how many*. Results are presented with numbers and statistical calculations. **Qualitative methods** are typically used when describing processes, with research questions starting with *how* or *why*. Results are described with words, and analysis involves text rather than numbers. For example, studies of parent–child conversations may apply quantitative analysis when counting words and sentence lengths, and qualitative analysis for investigating children's and adults' contributions in early dialogues. The choice of methods used depends also on area of interest. Both natural observations of children in their everyday environments and experimental studies have their place in developmental research. Infancy is a phase of great interest to researchers because it represents the beginning of many abilities and skills, such as **self-regulation**, self-propelled mobility and **communication**. However, it is not easy to instruct infants, and researchers would not get many answers just by asking them about their thoughts or feelings. Adapted methods based on **habituation**, visual exploration or neurological measures have given many new insights into perceptual and cognitive processing in infancy, but interpretation of the results of the studies can be challenging.

Reliable and valid methods are important in research, but they are equally important in clinical work. **Assessment** to gain knowledge about the thoughts and feelings of children and adolescents is a foundation of clinical work. The methods used depend on the age and assumed functioning of the child or adolescent. An assessment may, for example, seek to reveal a child's cognitive, linguistic and social functioning compared with peers, how he copes with emotional and stressful situations, and his relationships and interactions with peers and adults. Clinicians get information from conversations with the parents, the child and teachers and use systematic observation and standardized tests and checklists to investigate the child's performance in different developmental domains. The reason for an assessment is always a referral, and the aim is to find out if the child is in need of educational or psychological intervention, and what kinds of interventions will best support the child, the family and the school.

Atypical development includes all forms of unusual or deviant development, and there are many degrees of atypical development. Atypical development does not necessarily imply abnormality, but some children and adolescents have characteristics that fulfill the diagnostic criteria for one or several disorders, such as hearing impairment, **autism spectrum disorder** or anxiety. *Part IV Child and Adolescent Disorders* describes the characteristics of the most common disorders of childhood, based on the most recent editions of the two major classification systems: *The International Statistical Classification of Diseases and Related Health Problems* (ICD-11) and *Diagnostic and Statistical Manual of Mental Disorders* (DSM-5). The typical trajectories and developmental variation are described in the other topic books, together with their developmental consequences. For example, the development of self-propelled mobility gives children new ways of exploring the environment and thereby changes the whole psychological landscape of children, and, as part of motor development, Book 3, *Perceptual and Motor Development*, describes consequences of motor impairments on different aspects of development. The social functioning of children with autism spectrum disorder is discussed in relation to the development of **mind understanding** (Book 4, *Cognition, Intelligence and Learning*), while reactive attachment disorder and disinhibited engagement disorder are included in the presentation of attachment and development of early relations.

Atypical development reflects general processes, and knowledge about atypical development is therefore essential for understanding development in general. In addition, knowledge of typical and atypical developmental processes as bases for various disorders is important for understanding these disorders and for introducing appropriate intervention measures when needed.

The basic concepts and models, theoretical approaches, methods for research and assessment, and categories of disorders presented in this book constitute a basis for the study of child and adolescent psychology and a developmental way of thinking. However, a comprehensive understanding requires further study of the issues related to the various domains of child and adolescent development. The topic books and the complete textbook comprise all the main developmental domains of child and adolescent psychology.

Part I

Developmental Psychology

1

Psychology and Development

Psychology is concerned with human beings' (and animals') under-standing of the physical and social environment, and the bases for their actions, feelings and experiences, as well as their participation in greater and smaller social networks and in society. Developmental psychology is concerned with how all this comes about, how children gradually change socially, mentally and behaviorally, the underlying processes and the factors that may influence these changes, for exam-ple how children's understanding of the world and thinking changes over time, what makes children develop different abilities, how chil-dren form relationships with parents and peers, why boys and girls tend to play in different ways and come to have different interests and behavior, why some children are socially active and extrovert while others are more shy and careful, and how emotional expressiv-ity differs between **cultures**. Developmental psychology also includes the developmental courses of children with sensory and physical dis-abilities, as well as the **vulnerability** and risk factors that underlie the emergence of **learning disorders** and emotional and **behavioral disorders** in childhood and **adolescence**, and factors that may pre-vent the development of such disorders.

Development can be defined as an age-related process involving changes in the structure and functioning of human beings and animals as a result of interaction between biological structures, psychological states and ecological factors. While the organism adapts to its envi-ronment, the environment must also have properties that allow the organism to develop. At the core of the developmental process lies *transformation*: something new emerges, less becomes more, simplic-ity turns into complexity, limited skills evolve into advanced mas-tery (Overton, 2015). In all species, development toward adulthood

DOI: 10.4324/9781003291275-2

implies a greater degree of **autonomy** and independence from the parent, and in human beings and many other species also increasing social affiliation (Keller, 2016). The main characteristic of development is change, but in most areas there is both change and continuity. The individual develops new ways of understanding and mastering the world, but always building on past experiences and remaining the same individual (Nelson, 2007).

Development involves characteristics and abilities that are *common to all human beings*. Some are shared by humans and many other species, such as the ability to see, hear and walk, while others, such as talking and reflecting on the past and future, distinguish human beings. In addition, development entails processes that contribute to **individual differences**, in particular traits and abilities. Some changes are *quantifiable*, such as children's physical growth or the number of words they say. Changes in areas such as reasoning ability, social **adaptation** and moral formation are not quite as easy to quantify. They represent *qualitative* differences. The particular objective of developmental theories is to explain the emergence of new abilities and **qualitative changes**, both common and individual differences, and change as well as continuity (Kagan, 2008a; Spencer & Perone, 2008; see Part II Theoretical Perspectives, this volume).

With age, children engage in a growing number of activities and social relationships. They acquire the knowledge and values of their society and adapt to the physical and social cultural landscape, a process known as **enculturation**. Some children grow up in a conglomerate of different cultures, and their development reflects the multicultural background (Bronfenbrenner, 1979; Josephs & Valsiner, 2007).

The Historical Roots of Developmental Psychology

Psychology is a relatively young scientific discipline. Its origins are often dated to 1879, the year in which Wilhelm Wundt opened the first psychological laboratory in Leipzig. This marked the transition from largely informal observations to a more systematic methodology in the study of human **perception**, thinking, feeling and action. Nonetheless, most key issues in psychology are deeply rooted in philosophy and medicine, and many of its main topics can be traced back to ancient reflections on human nature. Until the late nineteenth century,

Ellen Key

child development was primarily an educational field, and literature on children mostly dealt with upbringing and education (e.g., Herbart, 1841; Rousseau, 1763). A few researchers, such as Tiedemann (1787) and Darwin (1877), described their children's development in detail, while Preyer published the first textbook with a general perspective on development in 1882. In 1900, Ellen Key proclaimed the twentieth century as *The Century of the Child*. It was equally to be the century of developmental psychology.

DOI: 10.4324/9781003291275-3

Developmental psychology encompasses widely different traditions that have moved toward and away from each other throughout history and influenced one another in varying degrees (see Part II Theoretical Perspectives, this volume). The theories reflect the knowledge that was acquired, but also the spirit of the age and the overall development of the society. Many attempts have been made to unite different perspectives, but there is still disagreement about basic developmental issues, such as the organization and biological bases of **cognition** (see Book 4, *Cognition, Intelligence and Learning*, Part I). Attempts at syntheses that integrate views from several directions and take into account the critique of others persist into the twenty-first century. Present day "developmental science" crosses disciplinary boundaries and integrates perspectives from developmental psychology with anthropology, sociology, linguistics, medicine and technology (Witherington, 2014; Zelazo, 2013).

3

Globalization

Globalization has become an integral part of modern societal development and has also impacted the development of scientific thinking (Valsiner, 2012). Early in the history of developmental psychology, Western European psychology was dominant, and, after World War II, American psychology assumed a leading role (Jensen, 2012). At the same time, theories were developed in other countries that did not always receive international attention. Vygotsky's influential book *Thought and Language*, for example, was first translated into English in 1962, 28 years after the author's death. Today the debate on development continues in Russia, but only a minor number of publications are translated into English (see Karpov, 2005; Vassilieva, 2010).

Cross-cultural studies are important for understanding the relationship between nature and nurture in development (see Bornstein, 2010; Nielsen & Haun, 2016). Similarly, cross-cultural discussions of scientific ideas are crucial to the advancement of developmental theories. For example, one-third of the world's children live in India and China, but, as neither country engages in much systematic theoretical work, India and China have little influence on international research in developmental psychology. In China, this is partly owing to the fact that psychology as a field, and individual-oriented psychology in particular, has essentially been an alien concept to the Chinese, a the group, rather than the individual, represent the natural unit in Chinese culture (Tardif & Miao, 2000). Moreover, during the Cultural Revolution (1966–1976), many psychology departments at universities were shut down (Blowers et al., 2009; Bond, 2010; Miao & Wang, 2003). In India, the British colonial powers had a considerable impact. Many of the studies involved children from upper-middle-class urban families, and generalization to other social classes

DOI: 10.4324/9781003291275-4

Development is global

is uncertain (Saraswathi & Dutta, 2010). Today, both countries are establishing traditions with a stronger basis in their own values and cultures. Also in Africa, psychology has been an article of import, but the number of studies founded on African ecologies and perceptions of reality is steadily growing. Here, too, an important discussion concerns the relationship between a universal and a local cultural understanding of developmental processes (Marfo, 2011; Nsamenang & Lo-Oh, 2010).

While globalization and English as the *lingua franca* of academia contribute to more equality in the development of theories across national borders, they also highlight the differences between countries and contribute to the establishment of unique cultural scientific identities. In the age of globalization, developmental perspectives with an origin in African, Asian and other cultures will emerge and find their position in international developmental psychology, both locally and globally. The coming years will show how these perspectives position themselves.

Typical and Atypical Development

Some children acquire certain skills and abilities early on, while others have a late or unusual development in one or more areas. A smaller group of children have disabilities or disorders that inhibit all or some aspects of development and have to perform many actions in unconventional ways. The most common course is **typical development**, with unimpaired functions and ordinary individual differences between children. Atypical development is a broad term used to describe all forms of irregular development, such as deaf children with a normal but unusual language development when they learn **sign language** instead of spoken language (Marschark et al., 2006), or children with **intellectual disability** who think and reason differently from their peers (Carr et al., 2016). Atypicality thus does not have to imply abnormality, only that something is done in less common ways. Knowledge of atypical development contributes to insight into developmental processes in general, and there is a long tradition of comparing the developmental trajectories of children with different prerequisites. Many early researchers included children with visual impairment, hearing impairment and intellectual disability in their discussions of child development (e.g., Luria, 1961; Piaget, 1970).

Every age level sees the emergence of abilities and skills that are particularly prominent or important for that age and form the basis for further development. Early skills and characteristics involve, among others, the ability to grasp objects, followed a little later by independent mobility and attachment to a primary caregiver, and then the development of language, understanding of minds, and morality. There are several ways of acquiring such skills and traits, both typical and atypical developmental paths. Children with severe mobility

DOI: 10.4324/9781003291275-5

impairments may need a wheelchair to explore their surroundings, but their **exploration** has the same function and importance as for children without such impairments (Anderson et al., 2013; Campos et al., 2000). Blind children usually show normal language development, even though they have to learn words with some other cues than sighted children (Pérez-Pereira & Conti-Ramsden, 1999).

It is the same basic principles that underlie all forms of development, regardless of whether it proceeds in an ordinary or unusual manner. Knowledge of typical development is necessary to understand atypical development, and knowledge of atypical development – of what can go wrong and how to compensate for impaired skills and abilities – is necessary to understand the developmental process in general (Cicchetti, 2013; Dekker & Karmiloff-Smith, 2011). The study of "**theory of mind**" in children with autism spectrum disorder and other disorders (see Book 4, *Cognition, Intelligence and Learning*, Part IV), for example, has been important in gaining insight into how children develop relationships and an understanding of how other people think and feel (Hughes & Leekam, 2004; Leekam, 2016). Most children with typical development will show positive development in quite different environments. Children with atypical development have a narrower range of possibilities and depend on an environment that fits their possibilities.

Recurrent Issues in Developmental Psychology

Many of the same issues appear in relation to descriptions and explanations of different developmental aspects.

Genes, environment and culture

The lay belief in genetic inheritance is strong, and parents typically point to similarities between their children and various family members. The role of heredity and environment in the development of individual differences is also one of the most discussed themes in developmental psychology (see Book 2, *Genes, Fetal Development and Early Neurological Development*, Part I). Another issue is the **universality** of abilities and traits. Some characteristics and abilities seem to evolve in regular patterns across cultures, while others differ from one culture to the next. For example, children of all cultures learn to speak, but they speak different languages. Comparison of how children develop in different cultures is an important tool for understanding the biological and cultural bases of abilities and characteristics, including cultural differences in demographics, nutrition and lifestyle. Cultural differences underline the fact that genes alone have limited value in explaining developmental processes. A somewhat related issue is to what degree research findings can be **generalized** across species. Similarities and differences between species can provide important insights into the developmental process, including the fact that there are a number of factors that cannot be generalized across species. Culture and language separate humans from other species (Nielsen & Haun, 2016).

DOI: 10.4324/9781003291275-6

Learning and development

Although **learning** and development are often considered opposites, they are not always easily distinguished. Both have to do with continuity and change in knowledge and skills, with becoming as a continuation or transformation of what is. "Learning" is generally defined as a relatively permanent change in perception and behavior as the result of experience. The acquisition of factual or other explicit knowledge undoubtedly qualifies as learning, but learning at school also leads to the formation of new **synapses** and brain circuits (Demetriou et al., 2011). Changes due to **maturation**, illness, injury or fatigue are not learning. Some theorists would argue that development specifically involves new learning based on previous learning, independent of biological factors. Others consider biological factors to be essential to the development process (Zelazo, 2013).

Continuity and discontinuity

Continuity means that there is a direct relationship between earlier adaptation and functioning and later ways of functioning. In **homotypic continuity**, form and function remain the same over time. Children and adults are both capable of running, but adults run faster. **Heterotypic continuity** means that the forms differ. One-year-olds stretch up their hands to be lifted onto mom's lap, while older children say Can I sit on your lap? to achieve the same thing. As early childhood involves major changes in children's behavioral repertoire, heterotypic continuity is most pronounced at this age. Differential continuity or **stability** means that children maintain their relative position with respect to their peers in terms of a particular ability or trait. A 2-year-old with frequent temper tantrums may have fewer tantrums at the age of 10, but relative to his peers he may be characterized by a short temper and behavioral disorders (Rutter et al., 2006).

Stages

Some theorists describe children's development as a sequence of stages, such as Piaget for cognitive development (Book 4, *Cognition, Intelligence and Learning*) and Kohlberg for moral development (Book 6, *Emotions, Temperament, Personality, Moral, Prosocial and Antisocial Development*). A **stage** is a period characterized by specific skills or characteristics and has to fulfill certain formal criteria. In the transition from one stage to another, children achieve a higher and qualitatively different level of competence than before. The transition must occur relatively quickly and involve concurrent changes in several areas. All children must pass through the stages in the same order. For most **stage theories**, there is disagreement regarding whether the stages actually meet these criteria (Lourenço, 2016).

Critical and sensitive periods

During development, there are periods where the child has a unique or particularly good opportunity for learning or development, or a particular vulnerability to harmful influences (see Book 2, *Genes, Fetal Development and Early Neurological Development*, Part III). An understanding of such **"sensitive"** or **"critical" periods**, from prenatal life to biological maturity, is important in order to prevent deviant development and initiate early intervention for children with developmental disorders. Related to this is a common view that experiences during early development are especially important and can install a form of vigilance or "preparedness," steer development in a certain direction and have long-term consequences (see Book 6, *Emotions, Temperament, Personality, Moral, Prosocial and Antisocial Development*, Chapter 16). Theorists disagree on the significance of early experiences, but both the positive effects of a sound childhood environment and the harmful consequences of growing up in poor or unsupportive surroundings are used as arguments in favor of early intervention (Bush & Boyce, 2014). For example, the first years of childhood are generally considered to be a sensitive period for communication and language development, and communication and language intervention is often implemented at an early age (Kaiser & Roberts, 2011).

Equifinality and multifinality

Flexibility is a characteristic of human development and children and can follow different pathways, both typical and atypical. **Equifinality** means that different developmental paths can have the same developmental outcome, such as the various ways of self-propelled movement prior to walking (Largo et al., 1993). Children who become competent language users can follow somewhat different development courses (Bates et al., 1988). Multifinality occurs when developmental paths with a common point of departure lead to different developmental outcomes. Some children with adverse experiences in the early years continue to have problems into adult age; others, with the same poor start, do well in adulthood. **Identity** formation during adolescence can take different paths for individuals who initially shared the same group affiliation (see Book 7, *Social Relations, Self-awareness and Identity*, Chapter 24).

Process and outcome

Some descriptions of development place emphasis on the outcome, on the various traits and abilities children usually have developed at different age levels and their intercorrelations, while others focus on the processes that lead to new traits and abilities, and the transitions from one state to another (Valsiner, 1987). However, the explanation of developmental outcomes must address the process itself, and an understanding of the process will provide the best basis for designing interventions for children who may be vulnerable to deviant development.

Multiple levels of analysis

Human functioning can be analyzed on a number of different levels (e.g., Gottlieb, 1992). Humans have genes and neurons; they perceive the environment through their senses, perform motor actions and mental tasks, and live in physical, social and cultural surroundings. Modern developmental science includes all of these various levels and the complex relationships between them (Zelazo, 2013).

6
Modeling Development

Developmental science seeks to model how biological and environmental factors affect children's development. A "developmental effect" will be the result of one or more influences. Developmental models distinguish between main effects and interaction effects, while **transaction effects** are the result of mutual influences between the child and the environment over time.

Main effects

A main effect is the direct result of an influence that is independent of other influences. A main effect can be caused by specific genes or environmental factors such as nutrition, exposure to certain events and so on. Eye color, for example, is exclusively determined by genes and the result of a main effect. Genetic disorders such as **Rett syndrome** and **Huntington's disease** are main effects (see Book 2, *Genes, Fetal Development and Early Neurological Development*, Part I); the presence of the disorders does not depend on other factors. An environmental main effect occurs when a sudden reduction in blood flow leads to brain damage resulting in motor impairment. The consequences of the impairment may vary depending on physiotherapy and other interventions, but the impairment itself cannot be "repaired." It may be argued that this is not development as such, but an external event with developmental consequences. Yet, there is no fundamental difference between this and other environmental influences: it is simply more dramatic than a condition such as malnutrition. In fact, it is precisely such dramatic events that may result in main effects, events that have such a pervasive effect on the course of development that other factors do not alter their effect.

DOI: 10.4324/9781003291275-7

Although a given trait can be the result of a main effect, a single factor alone does not necessarily determine the development of the trait, such as in the case of eye color. When several main effects act simultaneously, they are said to be additive. When trying to measure the extent to which height, intelligence, **personality** and other characteristics are the result of nature versus nurture, one usually proceeds from the assumption that genes and the environment operate independently, namely that two main effects (genes and environment) are added together (see Book 2, *Genes, Fetal Development and Early Neurological Development*, Part I).

Interaction models

An interaction effect occurs when the influence of a given factor is moderated by one or several other factors (Cicchetti, 2013). This implies that the effect of one factor cannot be determined without specifying one or more other factors. Figuratively speaking, **interaction** can be illustrated with the heat that melts the ice, causes the egg to harden.

Discussions about main and interaction effects are often concerned with the relationship between genes and environment. One example is when the gene variant determines the effect of characteristics of the environment (see Box 6.1).

This particular relationship is discussed in greater detail in Book 2, *Genes, Fetal Development and Early Neurological Development*. However, interaction effects can also occur between biological factors – including genes – and between several environmental conditions (Pennington et al., 2009). One example is when the relationship between a **difficult temperament** and the child's externalizing behavior is influenced by the mother's **self-efficacy** and her ability to manage the child's temperament (Coleman & Karraker, 1998).

An example of interaction between two environmental factors is demonstrated by a study that found a higher **correlation** between family income and children's academic performance in families with single parents than in those with two parents – good academic performance in children with single parents depended more on a solid household income (Zill, 1996). This may be owing to the fact that a family with financial problems has more resources to follow up the child's education when two are sharing the task than when a single parent struggles to make ends meet as well as provide the necessary help

Box 6.1   An Interaction Effect between Genes and Maternal Sensitivity

There are several different variants (**alleles**) of the dopamine receptor gene D4 (DRD4), each with a different number of DNA repeats. Forty-seven 10-month-old infants were observed with the mother in the home, and the mothers' **sensitivity** – how they reacted to their child – was assessed. When the children were 2–3 years old, the mothers completed a behavior questionnaire (CBCL) about their child. The children with the 7-repeat DRD4 and mothers who had been rated as insensitive were given higher scores for externalizing behavior than children with the 7-repeat allele and mothers who were rated as sensitive at 10 months, as well as children without the 7-repeat allele, irrespective of their mothers' sensitivity. For the whole group, there was no significant difference between children whose mothers had been rated as sensitive and insensitive; the effect is only observable if one differentiates children with and without the 7-repeat allele of DRD4. There was thus an interaction between the DRD4 allele and the effect of maternal sensitivity: only the externalizing behavior of the children with the 7-repeat was influenced by the mother's sensitivity at this age (Bakermans-Kranenburg & van IJzendoorn, 2006).

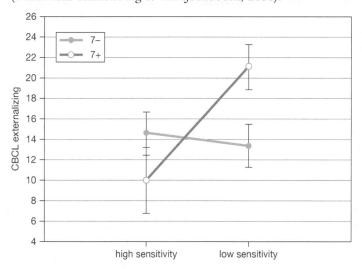

with schoolwork. Therefore, in order to predict how family income will most likely affect a child's academic performance, one needs to establish whether the child lives with one or with both parents. This shows that influences are not passively received, but integrated into the individual's own functioning, whether it be the influence of the parents on the child or vice versa (Rutter, 2005).

No aspect of child development is simple, and an explanation based on main effects is rarely sufficient. When taking a more detailed look at the factors that may underlie the development of a given trait or ability, one will nearly always find interaction effects (Elman et al., 1996).

Transaction models

Transaction models deal with the *mutual* influence between an individual and the environment over time. Descriptions of main and interaction effects generally focus on the influences on the child, but children also influence their surroundings (Bell, 1968). Extroverted children, for example, meet with different reactions from their environment than shy children. Children with Noonan syndrome, who are small in stature, are met differently than children who are tall for their age (von Tetzchner, 1998). Boys and girls are treated differently (see Book 7, *Social Relations, Self-awareness and Identity*, Chapter 27). Children with different temperaments elicit different parenting behaviors. Just as a father can react to a child with a difficult temperament in a way that helps the child achieve better self-regulation and development, a child with an **easy temperament** can influence her temperamental father to reduce the likelihood of his verbal or physical outbursts and become a better parent (see Book 6, Emotions, *Temperament, Personality, Moral, Prosocial and Antisocial Development*, Chapter 12). The experiences provided by the environment are thus not independent of the child, and a full understanding of the processes and conditions that shape the course of development must be based on how the individual and the environment influence one another over time. This requires a **transactional model** (Sameroff, 2010, 2014).

Figure 6.1 shows a simple transactional chain. Both the child and the environment change by mutual influence, so that the child's abilities and characteristics at various points on a timeline are the result of earlier development and new environmental influences, and the

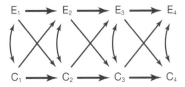

Figure 6.1 Transaction (based on Sameroff, 2009).

The transactional chain begins with the child and the environment at Time 1 (C_1 and E_1). The child's development at Time 2 is the result of the child's characteristics at Time 1 and the influences of the environment. The characteristics of the environment at Time 2 are the result of the environment's characteristics at Time 1 and the influences of the child. The child's development at Time 3 is the result of the child's characteristics at Time 2 and the influences of the environment, while the characteristics of the environment at Time 3 are the result of the environment's characteristics at Time 2 and the influence of the child. And so on.

environment is the result of existing characteristics and new influences from the child. The chain continues, incorporating both stability and change.

Transaction entails that the characteristics of the child and those of the environment constantly gain new significance during the development process. The developed child is affected by environmental factors. The environment changes as a result of the child's influence, and the child changes with each new environmental influence. A common example of transaction is the mutual influence between parents and children over time. At some point in the transaction chain, a child causes her parents to react in a certain way. The child is affected by the parents' reactions, the child's reactions and actions in turn affect the parents, and so on, in increasingly longer chains (Sameroff, 2010). The study in Box 6.2 found a transactional relationship between disobedience in infants, depression in mothers and behavioral disorders in adolescence (Gross et al., 2009). Another study found transactional effects between child externalizing behavior and maternal physical discipline (Gershoff et al., 2012). Studies show that maternal sensitivity to children with **fragile X syndrome** has an impact on language development, but also that the mother's sensitivity is dependent on the child's behavior (Carlier & Roubertoux, 2014; Warren et al., 2010). Hence, the child influences people in the environment who adapt in different ways to the child's characteristics as they perceive them. This in turn impacts their own influence on the child.

Box 6.2   An Example of Transaction Effects: Trajectories of Child Non-Compliance, Maternal Depression and Adolescent Antisocial Behavior (from Gross et al., 2009)

A sample of 289 children from predominantly low-income families were followed longitudinally from 18 months to 13 years. At 18 months, the mother–child interactions were observed, and instances of non-compliance and infant **aggression** were registered in situations that varied in stress, such as free play, clean-up, no toy and a short separation from the mother (see Book 7, *Social Relations, Self-awareness and Identity*, Chapter 4). The mothers completed a scale for depressive symptoms at several time points, and teachers completed behavior scales when the children were 11, 12 and 13 years old. The researchers found that higher levels of child non-compliance were associated with more persistent and higher levels of maternal depressive symptoms. Persistent but moderate maternal depressive symptoms, in turn, were associated with increased risk of adolescent **antisocial behavior**. However, it was not possible to predict adolescent antisocial behavior from toddler non-compliance. These results underline the dynamic interplay of transactional processes.

Ordinary age-related changes affect both children and adults. A 15-year-old is reprimanded differently by her parents than a 2-year-old or a child aged 8. Something that is forbidden by the parents and accepted by an 8-year-old straightaway may be perceived as unreasonably controlling by a 15-year-old. Similarly, parents often indulge toddlers who are stubborn or defiant, but react with anger and reprimands when older children behave the same way. Thus, a chain of influences can both be interactional and transactional.

The transactional model is a key element in the current understanding of development. The mutual influences between children and parents do not consist of isolated incidents, but interact with all the

Arnold Sameroff

other influences children and parents are exposed to. Children engage in interactions and relationships with their peers and adults, take part in events and activities in and outside of school and kindergarten and live under different physical and nutritional conditions (Wachs, 2003). Parents have different professions, engage in social relations in and outside of work and involve themselves in community activities to varying degrees. Society's values, laws and practices will impact children's learning and development, education and peer relationships, and the way in which children and parents influence one another (Bronfenbrenner, 1979).

Analyses based on transactional models are important when the results of empirical studies are "translated" to practical work with children. Sameroff (2009) describes the three *R*s of intervention: remediation, redefinition and re-education. *Remediation* aims to change the child's progress and may include all aspects of the child's functioning, such as nutrition, cleft palate surgery or special education for dyscalculia. *Redefinition* attempts to change the parents' subjective perception of their child. Parents of children with atypical development may have to learn to understand their child's temperament, thoughts and experiences, for example that blind children explore the surroundings with their hands (Fraiberg, 1977). This may involve assigning new "labels" to what the child is doing. The aim of *re-education* is to provide parents with information about the possibilities and limitations of a child with a particular disorder and how best to meet the child's needs. Parents of children with mobility impairments, for example, need to understand how the ability to move independently impacts the child's psychological space, exploration and attachment (see Book 7, *Social Relations, Self-awareness and Identity*, Chapter 4).

7

Dynamic Systems

Human development is complex, and it is difficult to describe even a small number of the conglomerate of interrelated processes involved. Dynamic systems models may be used to go beyond individual interactional and transactional processes and capture more of the complex reciprocal changes among different levels of organization (Cox et al., 2010; Sameroff, 2010). A *system* can be defined as any collection of "objects" or components that interact by way of certain causal relationships between them. A *static* system describes the relationship between components irrespective of time, while a **dynamic system** also incorporates changes in the components and their function over time (Burton, 1994). Development involves different elements and processes, and dynamic systems models are therefore particularly well suited to describe typical and atypical **developmental pathways** (Smith & Thelen, 2003; van Geert & Steenbeek, 2005). From a dynamic systems perspective, the ability to learn, for example, will gradually change as a result of the learning process itself and the situation in which it takes place, such as a physics lesson that includes instructions, tool use and explorative interaction together with the teacher. Changes in children's learning thus are not merely quantitative, but also qualitative. Children acquire more knowledge and learn to think more and faster, but they also learn to understand the world around them in constantly new ways (van der Steen et al., 2012).

An important characteristic of dynamic systems is *self-regulation*. This means that a child's inherent characteristics can change based on previously existing characteristics or "knowledge" without external influence. For example, children can form new concepts by reorganizing already acquired concepts and knowledge that so far have

DOI: 10.4324/9781003291275-8

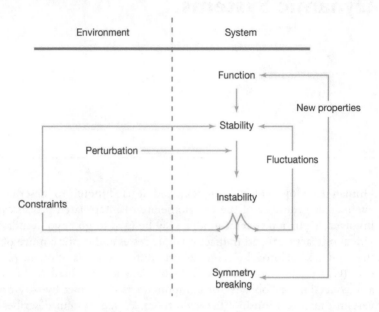

Figure 7.1 Dynamic model.

When the symmetry – or balance – between elements and processes in a dynamic system is disturbed, the resulting imbalance leads to the formation of qualitatively new characteristics. How the system behaves at any given time depends on the system's states at a previous point in time. Although the model does not include a timeline, the process of change always takes place over time (based on Hopkins & Butterworth, 1997, p. 80).

remained uncoordinated. When the system becomes unbalanced, it self-regulates based on feedback from the environment and the system itself, and influences on the environment and the effects of these influences. It is thus *imbalance* that brings change (Schöner & Dineva, 2007). Neither external stimulation nor a predetermined structure alone can ensure internal stability or the imbalance needed to bring about change in the system (see Figure 7.1). Imbalances can result in positive or negative effects, and the course of development can be typical or atypical.

Developmental models can be *linear* or *non-linear*. A linear system involves a proportional relationship between a phenomenon and the conditions it results from – between what goes into the system and what comes out. When such a relationship is not proportional, it is said

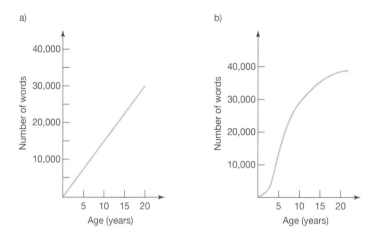

Figure 7.2 Linear and non-linear models.

The figure illustrates linear and non-linear models using a hypothetical growth in vocabulary. Model a is linear because the vocabulary increases by an equal amount each month until the age of 20. Model b shows a slow increase in vocabulary at the start, followed by a period of rapid growth; subsequently, the growth in vocabulary slows down, but without stopping completely.

to be non-linear. Supposing there was a linear relationship between children's vocabulary and their age: a 4-year-old would know twice as many words as a 2-year-old (Figure 7.2). This is not the case, however – the relationship between vocabulary and age is non-linear (Dale & Goodman, 2005). Most children begin to use words around their first birthday. Acquiring the first words takes a long time, followed by rapid growth during childhood and adolescence, and finally adulthood with increasingly slower growth, although the acquisition of new words never stops entirely.

An important characteristic of dynamic systems is their ability to integrate processes at different levels and allow for interaction between many factors and mechanisms. The development of walking, for example, can be described as the result of children's intention to move, their neurological and perceptual development, their motor and other physical prerequisites and the environmental conditions that make walking possible, such as a stable surface and something to hold on to for children who are not yet steady on their feet. In Piaget's theory, cognitive development is viewed as a continuation of the child's early perceptions, actions and general adaptation to the environment. Cognitive structures arise from the developmental process itself (see Book 4, *Cognition, Intelligence and Learning*, Part I). Dynamic models are based neither on the notion of development as fixed and predetermined nor on the assumption that all actions are shaped by the environment or based on imitation of an external model. They are not "deterministic" in the sense that there is a fixed relationship between input and output. Children's characteristics and actions are adaptive; they emerge from a complex and self-organizing system of physical, biological and psychological factors that can be either excitatory or inhibitory (Bates et al., 1998). The use of models capable of incorporating a wide range of different circumstances and details is problematic, however, in that they can become so extensive that little substance remains: the forest vanishes behind all the trees. A theoretical explanation is therefore called for when different factors are incorporated into one and the same model, and dynamic systems can be useful in generating new hypotheses about developmental mechanisms and relationships.

Cascades

The term "cascade" is closely associated with dynamic systems. It is used figuratively to describe how early traits or events lead to a sequence of stages, processes, operations or units. The outcome of one affects the next, leading to increasingly greater consequences across levels and for different domains at the same level (Cox et al., 2010). Inattention and restlessness in childhood, for example, can give rise to frustration, low self-efficacy and oppositional behavior. These in turn can lead to poor social skills, relational problems and learning problems at school, difficulties with boyfriends or girlfriends in adolescence and difficulties in the workplace in adulthood. One study found cascade effects from social adaptation in preschool and externalizing behavior in middle childhood on adolescent cognitive, social and behavioral functioning (Racz et al., 2017).

Developmental cascades thus describe the cumulative impact of multiple interaction and transaction effects in a developing system. Although each in itself could possibly have been prevented, together they may reach a scale that becomes difficult to handle. This proliferation of problematic effects over time is sometimes referred to as a "chain reaction" or "snowball effect." The effects can be direct or indirect, unidirectional or bidirectional and follow different paths. An important characteristic is that their impact is not temporary: a developmental cascade alters the course of development, and the result can be positive or negative (Masten & Cicchetti, 2010).

8

Vulnerability, Risk, Resilience and Protection

One of the main goals of developmental research and clinical work is to understand how various factors contribute positively and negatively to children's development. Some children have traits that make them *vulnerable* to particular developmental anomalies. A given environment can represent a developmental *risk* by not supporting a child's positive development or by directly counteracting it, and **disability** or injury resulting in unduly negative consequences. A typical environment will not always provide support for a positive atypical development. A severe hearing impairment, for example, always impacts the type of information children have access to as well as their ability to orient themselves in an acoustic environment, making interaction with others more difficult (Marschark et al., 2011). The consequences of a hearing impairment for a child's language development, however, will depend on the qualities of the environment, such as the availability and benefit of a cochlear implant (or other hearing aid) and a competent sign language environment. It is therefore essential to distinguish between an injury or a deficit of the organism and the resulting developmental consequences. An optimal environment cannot always be taken for granted. Children with **attention deficit disorder** are vulnerable to developing inadequate interaction strategies and social disorders. Structured activities together with guidance from parents and kindergarten personnel can have a protective effect and help them develop good social skills (Hinshaw & Scheffler, 2014). The timing of positive and negative experiences can be important, as the consequences of risk and protective factors depend on when they occur in the course of development. Children can be vulnerable or resilient at different times, for example during sensitive or critical

DOI: 10.4324/9781003291275-9

periods when they are particularly vulnerable to negative environmental influences or dependent on specific influences to be able to develop normally.

Figure 8.1 illustrates an interaction model of risk and vulnerability. The development process is determined by the interaction between the child's characteristics and those of the environment. Even if children grow up under environmental conditions that represent a significant risk of aberrant or delayed development, they will develop normally as long as they are not vulnerable to these particular environmental conditions. If children are vulnerable to specific environmental factors, they need an environment free of such factors for normal development. Most children grow up under environmental conditions that do not represent a significant risk based on their prerequisites

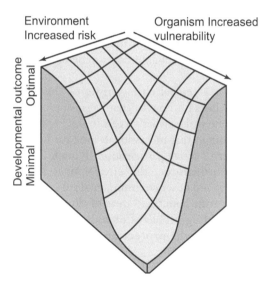

Figure 8.1 A developmental model of risk and vulnerability (based on Horowitz, 1987).

The figure shows the possible developmental consequences of the organism's vulnerability and risk factors in the environment. An optimal developmental outcome can be the result of invulnerability, absence of risk factors or both. An organism with low vulnerability is protected against risk factors in the environment. Without risk, vulnerability is immaterial. Therefore, a non-optimal developmental outcome will always be the consequence of a certain vulnerability of the organism and a certain degree of risk in the environment.

and therefore develop normally. A sensitive and responsive caregiver can counteract the negative effects of early and severe deprivation (McGoron et al., 2012), but, even under normal environmental conditions, some children with impairments or disabilities are vulnerable to a greater or lesser degree and will show atypical development under all or most environmental conditions, such as girls with Rett syndrome (Feldman et al., 2016).

In order to be able to prevent disorders in children, it is important to identify the factors and processes that may underlie vulnerability and risk. From a developmental perspective, it is natural to investigate the basis of children's positive development, also in the presence of vulnerability and risk factors. Even among children who are at serious risk of aberrant development, such as growing up in an unstable home environment and having little contact with trusted adults, there are always some who manage to cope relatively well. They seem to be "invulnerable" or resilient to negative influences (Garmezy, 1991; Luthar et al., 2014). **Resilience** is the complement to vulnerability and risk and results from the same developmental processes (Supkoff et al., 2012).

Resilience is not a general characteristic of children, nor does it provide clear guidelines for how to guard against problems. However, resilient children often take an active part in solving the problems they face, and it is important that professionals look for such characteristics and support children's active participation (Rutter, 2013; Seligman & Darling, 2007). Furthermore, the environment itself can protect against vulnerability and other environmental risks. Studies of children adopted from war-torn countries, areas of drought and famine, and from mothers with drug problems provide insight into risk factors, children's resilience and the **protection** offered by the environment (Palacios & Brodzinsky, 2010).

The model in Figure 8.1 illustrates important aspects of development. It is based on a diathesis–stress model that attempts to explain psychological disorders as the result of child vulnerability and stressful experiences. *Diathesis* is a congenital predisposition, and *stress* in this context is defined as negative experiences. The model deals exclusively with negative development or absence of negative development, however, and lacks promotive factors – positive development is merely the result of invulnerability and absence of risk (Roisman et al., 2012). Horowitz's model includes no positive forces and makes no allowances for resilience and protection. Furthermore,

Sameroff (2009) points to the presence of factors that promote a positive development, independent of any vulnerability and risk. In the same way that children differ in vulnerability to negative experiences, they react differently to positive experiences, for example praise (Brummelman et al., 2014; Pluess & Belsky, 2013). These are complex relationships.

9

The Developmental Way of Thinking

Developmental psychology comprises a wide range of issues, and, as has been shown earlier, complexity in phenomena and processes is an inherent characteristic of all human development. The developmental way of thinking is a central tool in both research and practical work with children and adolescents. Within a developmental way of thinking, the abilities and characteristics of the individual are not perceived as predetermined; they do not come ready-made but are results of complex interactions and transactions between biological and environmental factors over time. It is not a question of genes *or* environment, but of how these interact in the different phases of development. At any point in time, the individual's abilities, characteristics and functioning must be understood as both results of the developmental process that the individual has passed through and a basis for the development that lies ahead, that is, what the individual *is* and *will become*. There is a continuous process of organization and reorganization of abilities and characteristics, where the individual both changes and remains the same. A developmental way of thinking implies seeing children both as they are and what they are in the process of becoming from biological, social and cultural perspectives. Children grow and develop physically and mentally and are constantly becoming involved in new activities and relating to new people. Also, the extent and quality of these activities and relationships are changing. Within *applied developmental science*, the developmental way of thinking is a tool for adapting society to support children's optimal cognitive, emotional and social development (Lerner and Castellino, 2002).

DOI: 10.4324/9781003291275-10

A unifying conceptual framework of development – including what develops, how it develops, and what can hurt or help development – can give policymakers an understandable yet expansive framework that is anchored in science. When this framework replaces vague perspectives or models (e.g., child as blank slate), policy makers can use child development research to inform their decisions about policies and programs that serve children best.

(Hogan & Quay, 2014, p. 247)

Developmental Psychopathology

Developmental psychopathology is a multidisciplinary field that seeks to reveal and influence the processes that can give rise to mental problems in children and adolescents and uncover factors that can promote or inhibit the development of psychological disorders (Lewis & Rudolph, 2014). Rather than a theory, it is a perspective with significance for research and practice (Rutter, 2014). Building on a developmental way of thinking, mental health problems and the absence of such problems are viewed as consequences of children's vulnerability and resilience, and of risk and protection in the childhood environment. It seeks to explain the developmental process itself and thus differs from other approaches that place more emphasis on the presence of specific genes or traumatic experiences (Sroufe, 1997, 2007). One of the basic principles of this approach is that mental health problems do not arise spontaneously out of a void, but are the result of a developmental process. The roots of a disorder can go far back in time from the onset of symptoms and the establishment of a diagnosis. Toddler age, for example, can be a vulnerable period. At this age, children gradually become more mobile, but have yet to develop the cognitive skills to understand the consequences of their actions, as well as the ability to regulate their own emotions. Parents can find it difficult to deal with their child's behavior, and the first signs of internalizing and externalizing behaviors may begin to emerge. This may be the beginning of a developmental path with vulnerability of poor adaptation throughout life (Wiggins et al., 2015). To cite another example: usually there is a positive relationship between **empathy** and mental health, but a high degree of empathy can also increase children's worry and guilt and thus make them vulnerable to developing internalizing problems (Tone & Tully, 2014).

As **psychopathology** represents a deviation from normal functioning, its **identification**, diagnosis, treatment and prevention must be based on knowledge of the normal course of development. Developmental psychopathology integrates knowledge of typical and atypical development, maintaining that any adaptation or lack of adaptation throughout an individual's life must be understood from a developmental perspective, where biological, psychological and social factors can contribute to healthy development under normal or difficult conditions, as well as to the development of psychopathology. It furthermore places emphasis on uncovering how different developmental paths can lead to the same end state (equifinality), and how a particular vulnerability or risk can lead to various mental problems (multifinality). The goal of developmental psychopathology is to "translate" research-based knowledge into clinical work, understand each child's unique developmental path and facilitate preventive and treatment measures that allow children and parents to take advantage of positive developmental opportunities (Cicchetti & Toth, 2009; Rutter & Sroufe, 2000).

Summary of Part I

1 *Development* can be defined as age-related changes or transformations in the structure and functioning of human beings and animals as a result of biological and environmental factors. Development comprises characteristics that are shared by humans and other animals, characteristics that are common to all humans and individual differences, and change as well as stability.

2 Most key issues in psychology are deeply rooted in philosophy and medicine, and many of its main topics can be traced back to ancient reflections on human nature. Developmental psychology encompasses widely different traditions, and there is disagreement about many of the basic issues.

3 *Cross-cultural discussions* are important for the development of new knowledge. *Globalization* contributes to the development of theories across national borders and to a more diverse cultural perspective on the development process.

4 Most children have a typical development, with unimpaired functions and ordinary individual differences. *Atypical development* comprises all forms of unusual development.

5 *Main effects* are the result of an influence that acts independently of other influences. When several main effects act at the same time but independently of each other, they are said to be *additive. Interaction effects* occur when the impact of a given factor is moderated by one or more other factors.

6 *Transaction effects* are the result of mutual influences over time. Children are affected by the environment and affect the environment in turn. The environment changes as a result of the child's influence, and so on.

7 *Dynamic systems* models provide detailed descriptions of the developmental process. They *self-regulate* based on feedback from the

environment and the system itself, and influences on the environment and the effect of their impact. Regulation is brought about by *imbalance*. The term *cascade* is used to describe the way in which early traits or events lead to a sequence of stages, processes, operations or units. The outcome of one affects the next, leading to increasingly greater consequences.

8   All developmental theories make assumptions about characteristics that represent *vulnerability* in children or *risk factors* in the environment that can lead to aberrant development and developmental anomalies. Children may be *resilient* to stress, and environments may have qualities that offer *protection*. The *diathesis–stress model* describes **mental disorders** as the result of predisposed vulnerability and stressful life events. However, positive development can also be the result of promotive factors, independent of any vulnerability and risk.

9   *A developmental way of thinking* implies seeing children both as they are and as what they are in the process of becoming, from biological, social and cultural perspectives. *Developmental psychopathology* is a multidisciplinary approach that views mental problems and the absence of such problems as developmental consequences of children's vulnerability and resilience, and risk and protection in the environment.

Core Issues

- The role of main effects, interaction and transaction in modeling typical and atypical development.
- Usefulness and limitations of the diathesis–stress model.

Suggestions for Further Reading

Overton, W. F., & Lerner, R. M. (2014). Fundamental concepts and methods in developmental science: A relational perspective. *Research in Human Development, 11,* 63–73.

Rutter, M., & Sroufe, L. A. (2000). Developmental psychopathology: Concepts and challenges. *Development and Psychopathology, 12,* 265–296.

Sameroff, A. (2010). A unified theory of development: A dialectic integration of nature and nurture. *Child Development, 81,* 6–22.

Sternberg, R. J. (2014). The development of adaptive competence: Why cultural psychology is necessary and not just nice. *Developmental Review, 34,* 208–224.

Part II

Theoretical Perspectives

10

The Function of Developmental Theories

Part II provides a brief introduction to the foundations of theory formation and the most important theoretical perspectives in developmental psychology: **psychodynamic psychology**, **behaviorism**, *logical constructivism*, **social constructivism**, **evolutionary psychology**, *ethological psychology*, **ecological psychology**, **information processing** and **critical psychology**. They differ in their emphasis and explanations of developmental phenomena and together they illustrate the breadth of developmental thinking in the twenty-first century. Each of them comprises many assumptions and hypotheses, and constitutes a basis for many smaller theories.

The theories are presented in more detail in parts of the book where they are relevant, including critical comments. Book 4, *Cognition, Intelligence and Learning*, for example, discusses the cognitive aspects of the theories, while Book 6, *Emotions, Temperament, Personality, Moral, Prosocial and Antisocial Development*, discusses the development of personality.

Developmental theories are intellectual tools for categorizing and making sense of observations of children's actions and reactions and their environment and explaining typical and atypical developmental trajectories. As all tools, they must be functional and solid. A good theory requires a coherent set of interconnected concepts and a terminology that can be used to describe the development of the psychological phenomena and explain the relevant processes, for example concepts that can characterize children's changing thinking or emotion understanding, and the processes that underlie these developmental changes (see Books 4, *Cognition, Intelligence and Learning*, Part I, and 6, *Emotions, Temperament, Personality, Moral, Prosocial and Antisocial Development*, Part 2). "The usefulness of a theory may

DOI: 10.4324/9781003291275-12

be evaluated in regard to its attributes of precision, scope and deploy-ability" (Lerner, 2002, p. 11).

According to Popper (1959), a theory has to be testable in order to be scientific. The first test of whether a theory is sound and tenable is to establish if it can account for and integrate existing research findings (Lerner, 2002). Popper also points out that theories cannot be *proven* right, only wrong. A positive finding may be important but consistent with several explanations and unable to distinguish between even opposing theories. When findings contradict a hypothesis that is logically inferred from a theory, the theory must be revised or discarded. Negative evidence is therefore more decisive than positive in scientific inquiry, and when evaluating a theory it is necessary to ask what observations could possibly falsify the theory. A good theory must be able to generate hypotheses – statements about states of affairs that can be logically derived from the theory – that can be investigated in such a way that there is a potential result that would falsify the hypothesis and theory. If it is not possible to deduct hypotheses logically from a theory that will test its validity, the theory will remain speculative, even if it is both interesting and sounds reasonable. In addition, most theories include some hypothetical constructs that are not directly observable – such as the existence of internal working models

Richard M. Lerner

(Book 7, *Social Relations, Self-awareness and Identity*) or defense mechanisms (Book 6, *Emotions, Temperament, Personality, Moral, Prosocial and Antisocial Development*). Their existence can only be inferred through interpretation of observations, and the interpretation may require corroborating evidence.

In the same way as a theory needs evidence, research results need a theory to be useful in a scientific inquiry. Without a theoretical framework, results are empty facts without explanatory force (see Part III, Methods of Gaining Knowledge about Children, this volume). Practitioners also use theories when they try to explain the emergence of problems in a child who has been referred for example for severe social withdrawal or **bullying**. However, the dependence on a theoretical framework may also imply biases in the selection of observations and their inferences (Miller, 2011). To reduce the influence of such biases, both researchers and practitioners need to make their theoretical basis explicit and recognize their own possible biases when selecting and interpreting observations.

It is a major aim of research to distinguish between competing theories. However, because findings often are consistent with several explanations and theories, researchers may have to do many different studies before they can favor one theory over others – or abandon it. A theory may emerge from some basic assumptions, derived from observations of children, existing developmental theories and philosophical ideas, and gradually grow into a larger and more complex theoretical construction. Theory building goes through a kind of scientific evolution with survival of the fittest, with reciprocal influences between theory and research findings. In this evolution, those theories will survive that have fewer unobservable constructs and have been widely studied with few findings contradicting their hypotheses. However, even if a theory's predictions are contradicted on some accounts and the theory eventually is revised or abandoned, it may not imply that the theory has been useless. Many aspects of Piaget's cognitive theory have been contradicted by research findings, for example his assumptions about logic and stages in the development of thinking (see Book 4, *Cognition, Intelligence and Learning*, Part I), but the theory constitutes an invaluable foundation for the understanding of cognitive development because it has generated a lot of research questions and hypotheses. It has a clearly defined set of concepts and the most important feature of any theory – it can be tested.

11

Psychodynamic Psychology

Psychodynamic psychology has its roots in the **psychoanalytic theory** of Sigmund Freud (1916), but most of Freud's original assumptions have been reformulated or replaced by new theoretical constructs. Within the overarching psychodynamic framework, the disputes and differences of opinion are considerable, and there is no dominating psychodynamic approach (Luborsky & Barrett, 2006; Westen, 1998).

One knowledge base for psychodynamic theories is the causes of and treatments of psychological problems. Because psychodynamic psychology tends to assume that mental disorders largely originate in childhood experiences, clinically oriented psychodynamic theories also include assumptions about developmental processes. The other major knowledge base is studies of typical child development, often based on the assumption that psychological disorders reveal general features of development.

A central element of psychodynamic theory is the development of an *internal psychological structure* that determines the individual's perceptions of the world, actions and values. Individual mental functions are integrated into a coherent structure as part of the child's adjustment to the surroundings. Many psychodynamic theories maintain that the primary course of development is predetermined and universal, and that the formation of an individual's mental structure follows a set biological course. When complete, the personality has been shaped by individual experiences, but genetic predispositions determine what experiences are significant at different age levels.

All psychodynamic theories emphasize the child's relationships with other people and especially with the parents, but they have different assumptions about the motivational bases for these relationships. Freud (1905) argues that all human motives are derived from two innate

DOI: 10.4324/9781003291275-13

Sigmund Freud
Everett Historical/Shutterstock

drives: **libido**, the sexual or life drive, and **thanatos**, the hatred or destructive drive. The drives must be released, and children turn to their parents to satisfy their needs, for example for food or sucking. Children's future relationships with other people will depend on the ways in which their drives and needs have been met. At first, children are dominated by the **pleasure principle** and gradually adapt to the physical, social and cultural conditions that are necessary for reducing the drive levels and follow the **reality principle** (Freud, 1911). This development is made possible by the creation of a psychological structure consisting of **id**, **ego** and **superego** (Freud, 1927). In newborn infants, this structure is made up of the *id* alone; they are controlled by their drives. The *ego* enables children to pay attention to external barriers and limitations and adjust to the realities of the world. The third element, the *superego*, develops in later childhood and ensures that actions are not only realistic but also acceptable in view of the norms and values of the culture. The superego is shaped by the norms and values transmitted by the parents, typically the values and norms that the parents themselves received from their parents. The superego therefore represents a relatively conservative set of attitudes and values.

According to the classical theory, children's development is char-acterized by conflicts between impulses deriving from the id, ego and superego. All children will experience such conflicts to a greater or lesser extent, because parents make demands that cross the child's own **unconscious** and drive-based desires. Initially, conflicts arise between the child's wishes and external demands, for instance the parental insistence on cleanliness. Gradually, the demands are *internal-ized* and become part of the child's own restraints on its actions, and, consequently, conflicts between internal demands and internal desires emerge. According to Freud, it is the resolution of conflicts between the id and superego that forms the basis of the personality, although many psychodynamic theoreticians regard the ego as the most impor-tant structure, because the ego regulates impulses from the id and superego and adjusts to the surroundings.

Freud's theory of drives has been taken up by others, notably Melanie Klein (1948), whose basic assumption is that children are born with a conflict between life and death drives. She represents *object relations theory*, and, in the psychodynamic sense, an "**object**" is a mental **representation** of a person or thing that is construed as the goal of a drive or as a means for the drive to reach its goal. "**Object relations**" are **abstractions**, mental constructs of the roles the child and others have in interactions. Ronald Fairbairn (1952) argues that libido is not directed toward pleasure, as Freud thought, but toward "objects" – establishing relationships.

Other psychodynamic theoreticians are critical of the assumption that innate drives are the basis for the formation of relationships. Don-ald Winnicott (1960) rejects the idea that children's social relationships are dependent on a need to satisfy primitive drives and maintains that the wish to enter into relationships constitutes a drive in its own right. According to his theory, the relationship between mother and child is the natural unit in children's early development, and children only slowly become able to separate their own **self** from the union with the mother. Correspondingly, Margaret Mahler describes processes of *separation* and *individuation* where children gradually separate their self from the mother and become independent individuals (Mahler et al., 1975). In more recent psychodynamic theories, early interaction between mother and child is given greater significance, among others by Daniel Stern (1998) and Robert Emde (1998).

Another core assumption in psychodynamic theory is the presence of unconscious motives and behavioral impulses, which may surface in slips of the tongue and similar failures of control, as well as in symbolic acts. It is the interactions between unconscious motives that constitute the "psychodynamics." Children may experience anxiety when impulses to act or think come into conflict with their internalized demands. According to Freud (1894), children develop a set of **defense mechanisms** for regulating impulses and keeping anxiety at bay, making it possible for them to function within the community (see also A. Freud, 1966).

Ego psychology is an important strand within psychodynamic psychology. Among others, Anna Freud (1966) and Erik Homburger Erikson (1963) assign the ego an independent role in personality development. In the theories of Donald Winnicott (1965) and Heinz Kohut (1977), the *self* replaces the tripartite structure of the psyche (id, ego and superego), and conflicts between id and superego therefore do not have the same central position as in Freud's theory. However, development is still considered to be characterized by internal conflicts, and defense mechanisms remain a critical element in psychodynamic psychology (Westen, 1998). The developmental importance of mental conflicts is a feature that distinguishes psychodynamic theory from many other schools of thought and hinders integration with other theories.

According to Freud (1916), childhood experiences are critically important for the mature personality. He maintains that there is a relationship between the experiences during three **psychosexual phases** that children pass through before the age of 4–5 and certain **personality traits** or psychological problems later in life (see Book 6, *Emotions, Temperament, Personality, Moral, Prosocial and Antisocial Development*, Chapter 14). Erikson (1963) extends this idea in a theory of *social crises* that determine the development of normal and deviant personality traits. From yet another psychodynamic perspective, Stern (1998) describes how different aspects of the self are starting to be formed in different phases of development and remain independent but integrated parts of the mature person's **self-image**. At present, most psychodynamic theoreticians assign importance to events in early childhood but state that personality development continues well past **preschool age**, and that the personality can be changed, to a greater or lesser extent, throughout life (Westen, 1998).

Psychodynamic theories do not cover the full range of cognitive development, but the theory of a *tripartite consciousness* includes ideas about mental representations and memory organization (Freud, 1915).

The thought processes of the aware mind make up the *conscious*. The *preconscious* is made up in part of cognitive activity that may be, but usually is not, under conscious control and in part of mental representations that can be accessed, but only when the conscious mind focuses on them. The *unconscious* contains thoughts and feelings that are conflict-laden for the individual and enter the conscious only with difficulty, but still may influence the individual's actions.

Psychodynamic theory has two main methodological approaches. One is based on clinical practice and typically consists of detailed case histories that often are assumptions about development derived from treatment of adults. Furthermore, there are many different ways in which the internal workings of the mind can manifest themselves symbolically in behavior. Two identical actions may well have quite different underlying meanings. Freud argues that developmental psychologists may well miss important elements of development and misunderstand the significance of a child's actions unless they see them as outcomes of unconscious motives.

The other methodological approach is direct studies of children. Among others, Stern, Emde and Fonagy seek to fuse experimental methods of infant psychology with psychodynamic interpretation. Stephen Mitchell (1988) describes *relational psychoanalysis* as an integration of ideas drawn from object relations theory, self-psychology and infant research.

Psychodynamic theories have been of crucial importance for clinical psychology (Luborsky & Barrett, 2006). Although Sigmund Freud rarely worked with children, his theory dominated early child psychology to a greater extent than adult psychology, which has had to contend with several competing types of treatment. In the 1920s, Anna Freud and Melanie Klein began to develop psychoanalytical treatments for children. Psychodynamic developmental theory has also been highly influential on discussions about children's close relationships and their motivation, personality, identity and emotional development. During the last century, psychodynamic psychology has also had a major influence on ideas about how to bring up children, although always in conflict with behaviorism.

12

Behaviorism

Compared with other theories, behaviorism (also called *behavior analysis* or *learning theory*) attributes a greater role to learning processes. This does not mean that biology is without importance: behaviorism also assumes that humans are a result of evolution and biologically distinct from other species (Skinner, 1981, 1984). Genes constrain developmental trajectories, but learning is decisive, and all human functions can be explained on the basis of the same principles of learning, whether it be using language, solving problems, understanding emotions or entering into social relationships. Behaviorists often "translate" concepts from other theories – such as cognitive **schema**, attachment, **joint attention** and **social referencing** – into behavioristic terminology and explanations based on the relationship between stimuli and responses (Schlinger, 1995).

Behavior analysis concerns the relationship between behavior and environmental events. The environment is described as alterations of energy (stimuli) that reach the sensory receptors and trigger behaviors. Anything that the child reacts to in its surroundings is classified as a *stimulus*. A *response* is something the child does. Learning mechanisms include *respondent* (classical) and *operant* (instrumental) **conditioning**, and **imitation** (see Book 4, *Cognition, Intelligence and Learning*, Part VI). Behavior is regarded as an unbroken flow of actions that is constantly shaped, the incidence of actions increasing or decreasing in response to reactions in the environment. Sydney Bijou and Donald Baer (1961) define development as progressive change in the relationship between children's behavior and events in the environment. It is not the child who controls his or her own behavior; it is the surroundings that shape the child's responses (actions), and the responses are determined by the earlier learning history, that is, the conditions

DOI: 10.4324/9781003291275-14

Burrhus Frederic Skinner at the Harvard Psychology Department, circa 1950

which over time influenced the child's pattern of responding (Skinner, 1971). While the child's reactions to people around her might contribute to **shaping** particular behaviors, the final result will also depend on the *motivating operations* in the child, her physiological status as well as other situational factors (Laraway et al., 2003).

Behaviorism proceeds from the assumption that the same fundamental learning processes can explain all developmental changes, regardless of species or individual biological differences within the species (Skinner, 1938). The human species is characterized by an inborn *sensitivity to consequences* (Skinner, 1977). This ability is so general that it does not imply any specific **constraints** on behavioral development. In Skinner's view, a basic *survival drive* underlies all behavior and thus development. Learning enables the individual to survive in different environments, and children learn from experience without innate predispositions. Individual differences in behavior are mainly the result of differences in learning conditions.

Bijou (1968) describes three stages in child development that reflect changes in the biology as well as in the activities of the child. The *universal stage* covers the period from fetal life beginning up to the age of 2. Children's behavior in this stage is termed *ecological*, and there are hardly any cultural differences. The reason is not only that development is controlled by biological factors that all infants share, but also that children aged 0–2 tend to be treated in similar ways. The *basic stage* lasts from age 2 to 6. The biological development has reached a level that allows children to use more resources for investigation and acquisition of new skills and knowledge. Different surroundings, and thus experiences, contribute to individual differences between children and establish the behavioral basis for the third stage. The *societal stage* lasts from early **school age** onwards, throughout adulthood. Many different factors affect the child, expanding and altering the foundational behavior patterns. In many cultures, school plays an important role as it teaches children to read and count, complex problem solving and the history of the culture. At first, children's social participation at home, in school and with peers and others is defined by society, but control gradually passes over to the children themselves. Bijou emphasizes that the age ranges only provide an indication; there are

Albert Bandura

considerable differences between children with respect to the time they spend in the first two stages.

Albert Bandura (1978, 1986, 2006) is usually placed within behaviorism, although his cognitive or **social learning theory** differs considerably from traditional behaviorism. He emphasizes that people are conscious, goal-oriented managers of their own lives and includes explanations based on cognitive processes traditionally avoided by behaviorists. Still, Bandura also starts with the fundamental idea of development as a cumulative learning process and maintains that differences between children reflect different learning conditions. However, he puts more emphasis on *modeling* and **observational learning**, that is, children's ability to learn by observing or hearing about the consequences certain behaviors have for other people. This implies that observed consequences contribute to how children later cognitively regulate their own behavior.

Skinner's theory assumes that the relationship between features in the surroundings (stimuli) and behaviors (responses) is solely an empirical issue. Behaviorists have always been occupied with methodology. As the very name implies, analysis of observed behavior is the core methodological focus. Bandura (2001, 2006) extends the behavioristic perspective by including cognitive factors in explaining why children of different ages pay attention to certain aspects of their surroundings, how they interpret events and store and organize event information for future use, and why some events have lasting effects, depending on their perceived value and meaning. In Bandura's theory, learning is *goal-directed*. For example, children imitate people they admire or value, whether they are pop stars or friends, and such "reference people" change with age. Children's self-image and self-efficacy are also given much weight in explanations of why children act as they do. However, Bandura does not base his ideas on an assumption that children develop a cognitive structure of the type proposed by Piaget, but sees both social and cognitive development as outcomes of learning, as a continuous growth that gradually expands the child's behavioral repertoire and renders it more complex. Skinner and Bandura thus have quite different views on how new behaviors are acquired and maintained.

Behaviorism has influenced nearly all areas of developmental psychology, and its ideas have had a major impact on education. However, owing to the narrow explanatory system and resistance to "mentalist" concepts, behaviorism has made few inroads into the debates about cognitive and language development. Behavior therapy (BT) and applied behavior analysis (ABA), first developed by Ole Ivar Lovaas (1993), have had a large influence on interventions for children with autism spectrum disorders and severe intellectual disabilities. Bandura's cognitive theory has had considerable impact on personality and clinical psychology. Cognitive behavior therapy (CBT), which applies self-instruction and other cognitive strategies, is a common intervention for mood and behavioral disorders in children (Kendall et al., 2015; Mendez, 2017). ABA has influenced parenting, especially the focus on consequences of children's behaviors (Sanders, 1996; Webster-Stratton, 2006). *Super Nanny* and similar television series about raising children lean heavily on ideas from ABA.

13

Logical Constructivism

Logical constructivism is founded on the theory of Jean Piaget (1952, 1954). **Constructivism** assumes that children's understanding of the world does not depend on innate mechanisms but is constructed by the organism. Piaget's constructivism is called *logical* because his theory assumes that human thought follows logical principles. (Psychodynamic psychology is constructivist, too, in that the psychic structure determines how experiences are perceived and processed.) It was important for Piaget's views that his observations indicated that children perceive the world and its physical regularities differently from adults (see Figure 13.1). Hence, children are not small adults; their perception of the world is *qualitatively* different from that of the adult. They begin to perceive the world like adults only after a lengthy period of development, involving both innate characteristics and life experiences.

According to Piaget, development is a *process of adaptation*, of which the child's own **activity** is a core component. Children develop

Figure 13.1 Children's representations of reality

Children's drawings reflect the ideas they have formed about physical phenomena. When young children are asked to draw the water in a glass placed on a slope, they draw the line parallel to the top of the glass, and not horizontally as is the actual case.

DOI: 10.4324/9781003291275-15

Jean Piaget

knowledge and insight when they attempt new goals and have to overcome obstacles in order to reach them, for example move around a chair to get at a toy. Mental structures and processes are modified as children overcome challenges and acquire new experiences. They actively explore the environment, gain experiences and test the properties of the physical world. Piaget's vision of the child as active and creative was the critically important breach with contemporary views of cognitive development as the outcome of maturation and passive **internalization** of knowledge from adults.

According to Piaget, the cognitive structure provides the mental basis for all human understanding of and knowledge about the world. He compares it to a self-regulating (dynamic) system (see Chapter 7, this volume). Children exist in a state in which old notions are constantly challenged by new experiences and they will themselves seek out such challenges. If there is a *conflict* between new and existing ideas, the child experiences *disequilibrium*. The child solves the problem caused by a particular state of disequilibrium by altering its mental structure and thereby reinstating equilibrium. The new insight leads to new cognitive conflicts and disequilibriums. It is thus the cognitive conflict and the search for equilibrium which drive development. One example of conflict is if a child knows that two equal weights will balance a two-armed scale. He puts one weight on each side at random and discovers that the scale tips to one side. He did not realize that the distance to the middle matters and hence failed to take this into account when positioning the weights. The problem is solved by the child finding out that it matters how far from the center the weights are placed. By deducing that the weights must be placed at the same distance from the fulcrum, equilibrium is restored.

Piaget describes four cognitive stages characterized by qualitatively different functional capacities. At each stage, the cognitive structure sustains the logical **operations** that Piaget believes to be necessary to execute the tasks that children and young people learn to do at that stage. The stages are thus an ordering of children's developmental advances over time. However, Piaget's explanation of the developmental process is more important than the descriptions of stages, and especially what drives transitions from one level to the next, that is, cognitive conflict and **equilibration**.

Piaget's theory is still the only coherent theory of cognitive development and a starting point for almost all debate about cognitive development. Many developmental phenomena first described by Piaget, such as **object permanence** (that things exist when they are not perceived by the senses) and different forms of **conservation** (for example that the volume of water remains the same when it is poured from a wide to a narrow glass), are still central to descriptions of cognitive development. Some theoreticians use Piaget's theory as a basis, and others actively oppose it, but both are influenced by him (see Martí & Rodríguez, 2012). *Neo-Piagetians* such as Juan Pascual-Leone (1970), Robbie Case (1985), Graeme Halford (1989) and Kurt Fischer (1980) share Piaget's constructivist views and build on the ideas that children's functioning reflects underlying cognitive structures which become gradually more complex and better integrated as the child grows older, that structures which develop later build on previously developed structures, and that children are themselves actively engaged in acquiring knowledge and insight. They distance themselves from Piaget, however, in that they do not incorporate logic into the model (Morra et al., 2008). However, Pascual-Leone, Case and Halford integrate Piaget's theory and concepts from information processing theory, such as *mental capacity*, *processing speed* and **executive functions**. Most of the neo-Piagetians have abandoned the assumption about general stages but share Piaget's view that children's thinking undergoes qualitative changes in the form of cognitive reorganizations which may be described as a series of levels. Piaget constantly revised his theory and thus became himself a neo-Piagetian. In what has been termed **the new theory** (Beilin, 1992), both the stages and the base of formal logic have become less important (Piaget et al., 1992).

Lawrence Kohlberg (1981) has elaborated Piaget's theory on moral development. Kurt Fischer has used Piaget's theoretical framework to describe the development of emotions and personality (Fischer et al., 1990; Fischer & Connell, 2003), and the theory has been important in education (DeVries, 2000; Marchand, 2012), even though Piaget himself was not so interested in individual differences or whether his theory has practical applications.

14

Social Constructivism

This school of thought, which is also called *cultural-historical*, originates in the writings of Lev Vygotsky (1962, 1978). He is usually seen as an opponent to Piaget, but social constructivism distances itself just as much from other theories. Vygotsky actually shared many of Piaget's views, even though their main lines of argument have diverged. Both are constructive and have a main focus on cognitive development. According to Piaget, the construction is an individual project, while Vygotsky views the construction as socially mediated. Children's cognition is shaped through cooperation with others and internalization of **cultural tools** and thought patterns. *Internalizing* means that external processes, for example in formats such as dialogue and collaborative problem solving, are absorbed and become part of the child's mind. Children thus do not construct reality on their own. They are guided into the culture's activities and use of strategies and mental tools by more competent members of the society (children and adults), at first together with others and later on their own. Cultural tools such as oral and written language, numbers and mathematical symbols, art and maps can be developed only through cooperation with other people. They do not only help or facilitate thinking but change the cognitive organization and lead to qualitative changes in the child's cognition. Development thus consists in increasing internalization and increasingly complex handling of cultural tools.

Social constructivist theory assumes that children are born with biological mechanisms which also determine early cognitive development but that the individual cognitive resources are insufficient for the independent acquisition of the higher cognitive functions which characterize adults (Vygotsky, 1978). It is the influence of the cultural context which induces the biological organism to create meaning.

DOI: 10.4324/9781003291275-16

Lev Vygotsky

The basis for human consciousness and action is not to be found in the brain or the mind, but in external conditions of life – the social, historical and cultural expressions of human existence. Children depend on people who make the necessary mental tools and knowledge available and guide the children in using them. Enculturation happens first on a social, then on a psychological, level. Children's mastery includes both what they can manage on their own and what they can do with help from more competent persons (children or adults). It is precisely the "tasks" that children cannot do independently but can do with assistance from others which, according to Vygotsky, reside in children's **zone of proximal development**, and it is within this zone that learning can take place as a cooperation between children and adults. Mastery within the zone of proximal development implies that the child understands the task, but also that the adults adapt the assistance they give to make it useful to the child. Also, the help given must be within the zone of proximal development (Chaiklin, 2003).

Another main idea is that the cooperation between children and adults does not lead to abstract knowledge, independent of the context of the learning. Jean Lave and Etienne Wenger (1991) describe learning as *situated* within the activity to which the tools and strategies are relevant. Parents and children together take part in daily routines during which the child acquires different kinds of knowledge, for instance about lullabies at the bedside, food in the kitchen and wood in the workshop. It follows that acquisitions of specific skills depend on children taking part in interactions that have the necessary features.

Vygotsky describes four stages in development characterized by qualitatively different functional capacities. In these stages, children internalize cultural tools, develop more complex modes of thinking and integrate language and intellect. Vygotsky and Elkonin describe six phases in children's participation in activities, ranging from the first year of life, when the child joins in activities that typically provide intuitive and emotional contact between child and adult, to adolescence and the acquisition of vocational skills (Thomas, 2005).

Vygotsky's premature death at 38 years has meant that many of his theoretical ideas remain incomplete and unclear. Russian *neo-Vygotskians* such as Aleksei Leontiev, Alexander Zaporozhets, Piotr Galperin and Daniil Elkonin criticize several aspects of Vygotsky's theory, but also carry his ideas forward in **activity theory** (see Karpov, 2005). According to these theoreticians, children go through **developmental phases** characterized by various *main activities*, with their specific *motives*, *goals* and *actions*. Early on, one motive is to join in emotional interactions, while in adolescence one motive is to reflect on the self. In each phase, children have motives and behavioral resources which are appropriate for participation in the main activity but which they cannot manage on their own. The developmental phases are therefore characterized by activities which children and adults do together, with the adults acting as mediators. It is the mediation of the adults that drives development. When the adult has completed the mediation tasks in one phase, the child masters new mental tools and, together with the adult, is ready to enter into a new phase with main activities involving motives, goals and actions – and, once more, the child will need the adult's help to manage. In this way, activity theory represents at the same time extension, modification and revision of Vygotsky's ideas. Outside Russia, Michael Cole, Barbara Rogoff, Jaan Valsiner and James Wertsch are leading proponents of this school of thought. Much of the research has been concerned with cognitive and language development, but social constructivist theories have influenced most areas of developmental psychology, including development of moral (Tappan, 2006), self (Stetsenko & Arievitch, 2004) and identity (Hammack, 2008), as well as developmental neuropsychology (Akhutina, 2003) and education (Kozulin et al., 2003). They have also inspired critical psychology (see Chapter 19, this volume).

15

Evolutionary Psychology

Evolution is central to the understanding of how children develop. All developmental theories assume that abilities and skills may have a genetic basis. It is also a common point of view that children who are alive today carry genes which, during evolution, conferred the possibility of developing characteristics that "fitted in" with their surroundings and increased their survival chances, and that many human characteristics can be explained by the significance they had in the evolution (see Book 2, *Genes, Fetal Development and Early Neurological Development*, Chapter 4). However, evolutionary psychology assumes to a larger extent than other theories that psychological traits and behavioral tendencies are based on specific neurological mechanisms, **modules**, shared by all humans (Barrett & Kurzban, 2006; Lickliter & Honeycutt, 2015). The evolutionary process has been used to explain the development of aggression and altruism (Kurzban et al., 2015; Wilson, 1975). Steven Pinker (1994) writes about a "language instinct" that makes language a human biological necessity (unless brain damage has occurred in areas which the relevant genes helped to shape). There is no clear distinction between **nativism** and evolutionary psychology, and they are therefore presented together.

According to nativism, children are born with **core knowledge** in many areas, and development proceeds according to a plan represented in the genes (Carey, 2011; Spelke & Kinzler, 2007). Stimulation is usually necessary for activating the innate structures, but experiential differences have little influence on the developmental outcome (Scarr, 1992). Nativists assume that children are born with **mental models** which correlate with many aspects of the world, that a newborn's brain already "knows" how to go on to perceive

DOI: 10.4324/9781003291275-17

certain types of stimuli and events in its surroundings. The argument is that experiences are not in themselves sufficient to provide a child with reliable knowledge about the world or how to relate to people. The child's own mind must be able to contribute already *before* assimilating experiences, thereby transcending knowledge imparted directly by external stimuli. For instance, Noam Chomsky (2000) and Steven Pinker (1994) believe that language acquisition would be impossible without a language module capable of limiting the ideas children might form about the functions of speech sounds or of the hand movements in sign language (see Book 5, *Communication and language*, Chapter 6). Others maintain that infants are born with modules for face perception, numbers, spatial relationships and naive psychology (understanding of human relationships and feelings) (Spelke & Kinzler, 2007). An inborn mechanism that enables social learning by imitation has been suggested (Rizzolatti, 2005), and temperament and personality are also assumed to have a genetic basis (Buss & Penke, 2015).

That the basis for some characteristics has emerged as part of evolution however does not mean that they are independent of the individual's environment, only that a certain set of genes must be present for the individual to exhibit these traits. Genes make experience possible, and experience allows the genes to function (see Book 2, *Genes, Fetal Development and Early Neurological Development*, Part I).

There is considerable disagreement within evolutionary psychology with regard to the specificity of the neurological bases for human cognitive functions. Many argue, like Pinker (1997), Carruthers (2006, 2008) and Cosmides and Tooby (1994), that humans have a large number of specialized neurological modules because evolutionary adaptations require specific solutions. On the other hand, Bjorklund and Pellegrini (2002) maintain that human evolution implies the development of both modular and more general neural structures that enable adaption to different ecological niches. To suppose that evolution has created general neural structures is uncontroversial and in line with developmental theories in general. It is the assumption that many human functions to a large extent are determined by genes which distinguishes evolutionary psychology from other theories.

Nativism has influenced thinking about most areas of development, from motor skills and object perception to emotions and personality. Evolution has been thought to explain, for instance, sexual identity, criminality and violence (Buss & Duntley, 2011; Durrant & Ward, 2012). During the last 50 years, research that shows infants to be more competent than previously thought has had considerable influence on the field. In the twenty-first century many nativist views have considerable support.

16

Ethological Psychology

Ethology is the study of animals in their natural setting. The basic idea of Robert Hinde (1992) and other ethological psychologists is that understanding of the development and adaptation of the human and other species has to be based on knowledge about their biological capacities, the ecological niche in which characteristics have evolved and the ecological niche in which individual humans find themselves at present.

The ethological tenets influence the research methods. Ethologists prefer a natural science approach and emphasize the importance of describing children and young animals in different situations. One example is the observation by Konrad Lorenz (1935) that many young birds tend to follow whatever they first see moving within a time window which opens just after they hatched (**imprinting**). This makes it likely that they follow the mother and get food and protection and thereby increases the survival of the species (see Book 7, *Social Relations, Self-awareness and Identity*, Chapter 2). In the theory of John Bowlby (1969, 1973, 1980), children's **attachment behaviors** are regarded as having the same function as imprinting in birds. Children with genes that contribute to their development of attachment behavior and physical proximity to a caregiver have increased likelihood that they will survive to sexual maturity and thereby transfer their genes to other individuals.

Bowlby's theory is the major theory within ethological psychology and has contributed decisively to shaping the insights of contemporary developmental psychology into the early social relationships of children (see Book 7, *Social Relations, Self-awareness and Identity*, Chapter 2). It has had a strong influence on clinical psychology, social work with children and attitudes to raising children in general. It has also been an inspiration for ecological psychology.

DOI: 10.4324/9781003291275-18

17

Ecological Psychology

Ecological developmental psychology sets out from the premise that children are part of various social and cultural contexts, which they are affected by and also affect. Urie Bronfenbrenner is the key theoretician, and his *bio-ecological theory* is made up of four elements – process, person, context and time – which are integral components of a model for development (Bronfenbrenner, 1979; Bronfenbrenner & Morris, 2006).

In Bronfenbrenner's theory, *proximal processes* include the interactions between the individual and the environment. He views development as an outcome of interactions over time between the active child and human beings, objects and **symbols** in the immediate surroundings, which invite attention, exploration, manipulation, elaboration and imagination. Children become more capable with age, and therefore the proximal processes must grow too. The activities in which children take part become more time-consuming and more varied, and development thus involves both the individual and the group.

The person is an individual's biological, cognitive, emotional and behavioral characteristics. Every individual has three sets of properties: first, predispositions that can initiate the proximal processes within a specific domain and in a defined situation or context; second, resources such as talents, experiences, knowledge and skills that are essential for the effective function of proximal processes at a given point in development; and third, demands that either promote or hinder reactions from people in the environment which can affect the proximal processes negatively or positively. Inspired by Kurt Lewin's (1931) concept of "life space," Bronfenbrenner points out that the environment has both objective and subjective elements. The way in which a child is influenced by the environment, and influences

DOI: 10.4324/9781003291275-19

it in turn, depends on the subjective understanding, which reflects the child's experiences, including the emotional aspects of the experiences. The person's characteristics contribute in their various ways to individual differences in development. Moreover, they are included in the definition of the microsystem (see below), such as characteristics of the child itself, the parents, siblings, friends, classmates and other significant persons.

The context consists of a hierarchy of four ecological levels, or systems, which combine to create the environment in which the child grows up (Figure 17.1). The **microsystem** is an individual's situation at a given time in his or her life and consists of the relationships between the child and his or her surroundings. There are many microsystems, which interact and form a **mesosystem**. The mesosystem is the individual's developmental niche at a certain point in time and consists of the set of situations that are most important to that individual. How children function within their family and other significant environments affects how they function at school and with friends, and their school experiences affect the family situation. The **exosystem** comprises situations in which the child does not have an immediate role, but which all the same influence the child's behavior and development. The parents' employment situation, opportunities for holidays, social support, personal social network and other such factors (the exosystem) influence the care setting of the child as well as the functioning of the family (the microsystem). The parents of a child's friends (the exosystem) may matter to the interaction between the child and her friends (the microsystem). The **macrosystem** is a superordinate level and incorporates culture, community institutions and politics. The laws of the country (the macrosystem) regulate the organization of nursery schools and schools, and working conditions in general (the exosystem). They include duties, opportunities and rights which affect parents' care of their children (the microsystem). The influences also operate in the other direction: events in one or several families, nursery schools or schools (in the micro- and mesosystems) can lead to changes in the laws and social attitudes (the macrosystem). The four levels interact, and what happens at one level relates to what happens elsewhere.

The ecological systems represent stepwise extensions of children's environment. As children grow older, their social networks expand and become more complex. Children who live in the same country have the same macrosystem. Children who live in the same local area

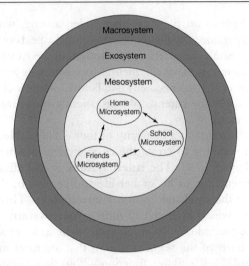

Figure 17.1 Four ecological levels (based on Bronfenbrenner, 1979).

Microsystem: consists of a child's intimate, daily relationships. In the Western world, these are usually with parents, siblings and other relatives who live with the family, as well as nursery school, school, after-school clubs and groups, friends in the neighborhood and similar.

Mesosystem: consists of links between two or several of the microsystems in which the child actively participates.

Exosystem: the wider social context in which the child is not active, but which matters for the functioning of the family and the child. It includes the parental places of work and their social networks, distant relatives, the parents of friends and similar.

Macrosystem: consists of social institutions, official services and similar, and includes the laws, customs and values of the society which affect the other systems.

are likely to share much of the same mesosystem, and also the exo-system if their parents often interact. It is, however, the mutual influences between all four levels which constitute an individual child's unique developmental environment. Besides, changes will take place, with time, at each level and also in the interactions between the levels. A child's world might come to include several siblings, or its parents might divorce and find new partners. Society's laws could change, as could its attitudes and values, changes which might deeply affect all four ecological levels.

Time is important in the bio-ecological model because the interactions must occur frequently over a period of time and are linked to the micro-, meso- and macro-levels. *Microtime* defines beginnings and ends of episodes of proximal processes. *Mesotime* is structured from such episodes, stretching over time intervals of days and weeks. *Macrotime* encompasses changes in expectations and events with lifelong or generational durations.

The bio-ecological model of development thus concerns interactions between a child and its environment which take place at different levels and with different time spans, and integrate the ecological systems and person characteristics within the framework of the transactional model (see Chapter 6, this volume).

Developmental psychology has mostly concentrated on close family relationships – especially that between mother and child. Bronfenbrenner's theory has contributed to a shift in research to pay greater attention to children's development within a wider social and societal framework. The theory is important for social and health care practice, and community-oriented work in general (e.g., Ashiabi & O'Neal, 2015; Benson & Buehler, 2012). Moreover, it has helped to clarify the influence that higher-order political decisions can have on the development of individual children and hence why political decisions should be included as relevant environmental goals (Golden et al., 2015) and as starting points for studies of children's development.

18

Information Processing

Theories based on information processing describe mental phenomena as information from the senses or memory being processed in various ways, and with various aims, including understanding of intentions and emotions, thinking and problem solving (Massaro & Cowan, 1993). Figure 18.1 describes a simple model of information processing. The computer serves as a conceptual **metaphor**: mental phenomena are calculations, and cognitive development is changes in how calculations are made (Simon, 1962); from this perspective, computer simulation of mental processes is an important research strategy (Schlesinger & McMurray, 2012). All mental functions are seen as involving the same set of processes, and both the number of processes and their capacity are limited.

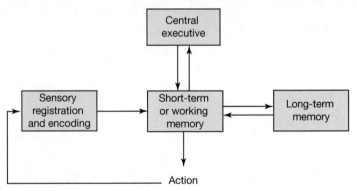

Figure 18.1 A simple model of information processing (based on Richardson, 1998).

The components act in conjunction when executing complex tasks, and the model can be used for different types of information.

DOI: 10.4324/9781003291275-20

Information processing is used to explore what processes are active when children manage different tasks; how the children encode and process information, **discriminate** between new and old information, and create concepts about people, animals, objects, emotions and so on; and how the processes change over time. The theoreticians agree that differences in the information and the ways it is processed can explain social and cognitive differences between children and adults. There is however considerable disagreement about *what* it is that changes. According to Pascual-Leone (1970), developmental changes are due to maturation-dependent increases in processing speeds and capacities, while Kail and Bisanz (1992) argue that the processes are constant and hence not susceptible to change. Michelene Chi (1978) represents a third view, that it is the organization of knowledge that changes. An "expert" in a particular area organizes knowledge differently to a novice. In addition, children learn new *strategies*. For example, children as young as 18 months can point to or name concealed objects in a hiding game, but lack strategies for hiding things. Five-year-olds place objects in the corners of the room and in other obvious places which allow them to be easily found. Another example is that children as a rule begin to count on their fingers and gradually learn new strategies for adding and subtracting which can be used also with numbers greater than the number of fingers on both hands (Kail & Bisanz, 1992).

Models based on information processing are becoming increasingly influential in developmental psychology, especially in typical and atypical cognitive development (see Book 4, *Cognition, Intelligence and Learning*, Part I), but other developmental areas also apply information processing models. The model of Crick and Dodge (1994) for processing *social information* has contributed to the understanding of the development of social functioning, personality and psychological problems by analyzing, for instance, how aggressive or shy children or children with ADHD process social information, and it is often applied in clinical work with children with behavioral disorders (e.g., Adrian et al., 2010; Fontaine, 2010; King et al., 2009). The process analytical approach of information processing is used in both mainstream and special education (van Nieuwenhuijzen & Vriens, 2012; Ziv, 2013).

19

Critical Developmental Psychology

Most of the developmental theories discussed are founded on a developmental way of thinking. Despite their many differences, they share assumptions about regular and age-related changes *within* children which result from interactions between biological processes and environmental conditions. However, in the wake of radical social constructivism and gender studies, *critical developmental psychology* (also called *psychology of childhood*) has emerged, influenced by postmodern sociology and psychoanalytical ideas about interpretation and comprehension (Morss, 1996). Erica Burman (2008, 2017) aims to "deconstruct" developmental psychology and insists that there are no independent individual developmental processes – they are only a construction in the minds of developmental psychologists (see also Callaghan et al., 2015). "Critical" theoreticians argue against biology-based development and are particularly critical of evolutionary psychology. They argue that assumptions about regularities in the development of children's inner processes should be replaced by an understanding of children's thinking and actions as products of the social and cultural contexts in which the children take part, and not any assumptions about their internal functions being different to those of adults (Burman, 2001, 2013a). Similarly, Dion Sommer (2012) focuses on *childhood* rather than on the abilities which emerge from within the child. In his view, it is the *cultural histories* that define childhood, who children are, why they are the way they are and their positions in society. Critical developmental psychology considers its main task is to expose, in political and social terms, the implications and consequences of the other developmental theories. Burman (2013b, 2017) maintains that the traditional schools of thought in developmental psychology have emerged as a result less of scientific research

DOI: 10.4324/9781003291275-21

than of historical, economic and political conditions, especially the position of women and their function as a source of labor, and that these theories, as a consequence, help to underpin the current social system in the West. Critical psychology stresses the importance of gender as a cultural variable, but largely disregards age.

Critical psychology crucially insists that knowledge about development is not cumulative but constructed within a particular historical and cultural context and hence is only valid at that particular point in time. When changes take place in the social and cultural attitudes to children, previously acquired knowledge about them becomes invalid and must be revised. This contradicts the established scientific view that knowledge accumulates as part of an "evolutionary" process where some assumptions are not supported and hence are abandoned, and others are supported and become accepted knowledge. For instance, it has been known for a long time that children start speaking during their first year of life. In medieval times, it was assumed that children would begin to speak even if they didn't hear speech, an assumption that is no longer accepted (O'Neill, 1980). In traditional developmental science, it is not the children who change throughout history but theories and empirical knowledge. In critical psychology there is no accumulated knowledge; children change when the theories change, because both are social constructs (Burman, 2017; Morss, 1996).

The critical perspective represents a radical break with the very foundation of developmental psychology, not least because it rejects the established understanding of the concept "development." There are relatively few critical psychologists, and the critical approach has had only a limited influence on developmental psychology and the study of children. It has had more influence on the understanding of *childhood* as a sociological phenomenon, and especially in relation to variation in family structure and **gender roles**. However, questions raised by this perspective have been useful as counterweights to established views in developmental psychology and have contributed to a more holistic appreciation of children in a social setting.

20
Distinguishing between Theories

This brief introduction demonstrates the considerable variation in theoretical approaches to developmental psychology, but also the many facets of children's capacities and the complexity of the developmental process. The theories differ but also encompass many similarities in their ways of describing development as a process of adaptation. Piaget (1952) and Freud (1916) both emphasize *conflict* as a driving force in development, but very different forms of conflict. In Piaget's theory, the conflicts are between elements of the child's perception of its surroundings, and the conflicts lead to **integration** of knowledge and cognitive development. In Freud's theory, the conflicts arise from children's motives and their demands on themselves, and the outcomes of the conflicts contribute to shaping personality. Freud (1930) and Vygotsky (1978) are both concerned with *culture*, but, in Freud's theory, culture represents distress to the child, something to which he must conform contrary to his own desires. Vygotsky (1978) sees culture as a positive component in development which enables thinking beyond the individual's own experience. Both also see *internalization* as an important mechanism, but in Freud's theory it is a case of internalizing external demands, while in Vygotsky's theory it is the acquisition of cultural skills and insights. Both Winnicott (1960) and Wertsch (1991) regard mother and child as a natural developmental *unit*, but for Winnicott this is a matter of mental representation, and for Wertsch it is one of collaboration to solve intellectual problems.

Theories differ in what factors they regard as more significant for children's development, but also, to some extent, in what aspect of development they emphasize. None of the theories can be said to cover the process as a whole. For instance, Piaget is particularly concerned

DOI: 10.4324/9781003291275-22

with the development of cognition and morality, both of which he regards as part of typical development. Freud was more interested in the development of personality and identity and had a clinical orientation, but also presents his ideas as elements within a generalized theoretical model of development. Different theoretical views may thus neither agree nor disagree, but rather focus on different aspects of development. For instance, Piaget's views were clearly influenced by Freud in areas which are relatively peripheral to his theory, and he was for some time a member of the International Psychoanalytic Association. In his first book, Piaget writes: "Correspondingly, my indebtedness to psychoanalysis should be quite obvious. I believe these ideas to have revolutionized the primitive thinking in psychology" (Piaget, 1959, pp. xx–xxi). Psychodynamic accounts usually include a Piagetian approach to cognitive development.

New hypotheses often have their origin in some kind of behavior observation, and there may be consensus about what children do and what happens in a situation. It is the interpretation of the observation, the assumed motives and precursors, and the conclusions reached that differentiate the theories. A shared observational basis sometimes makes it difficult to decide which of several competing theories comes closest to the truth. For instance, there is general agreement that some children are very shy and withdrawn, but disagreement about the reasons why children behave in this way. Behavioristic explanations would search for adult reactions to the child which may have contributed to maintaining the shy behavior. Cognitive learning theorists would, in addition, seek to gain insight into the child's self-image and self-efficacy. An ethologically oriented researcher may look for causes in the child's temperament and attachment relations. Finally, a traditional psychodynamic researcher may try to reveal unconscious psychological conflicts that have complicated the child's relationships with the mother and father.

When it becomes hard to discriminate between two contradictory but reasonable interpretations, both may be considered valid until there are grounds for excluding one of them. The theoretical selection process is however made more difficult still by the potential disagreement about the scientific basis and research methodology. Consequently, some of the knowledge remains uncertain and fragmented. Discussions about developmental psychology are characterized by phrases such as "on one hand . . . but on the other." A developmental way of thinking is a tool for reflecting on uncertain theoretical and methodological circumstances, as well as professional dilemmas during clinical work with children.

While studying developmental psychology, it may be useful to start by focusing on the phenomena – on what observations, experiments and other investigative approaches may tell about children. Once the phenomena are described, the next steps in the exploration of children's development are to compare the explanations and interpretations, identify the issues about which theories agree and disagree, and clarify their compatibility, that is, whether both could be true or if one excludes the other. The truth is not likely to be found somewhere halfway between two perspectives. Many theoretical views simply cannot be united: acceptance of one view will imply that other views must be rejected. A theory must be wrong if evidence supports a contradictory theory. And, often, there is no definite answer: one simply does not know which theory is the right one.

Summary of Part II

1 Developmental theories attempt to explain the changes that take place between conception and adulthood. Modern developmental research has followed several different lines of thought, and there is considerable variation between ideas and views within each perspective.

2 A good theory requires a coherent set of interconnected concepts and must be able to generate hypotheses that can test its validity.

3 *Psychodynamic psychology* is rooted in Sigmund Freud's psychoanalytic theory. Main elements are the importance of the *early years*, an *inner psychic structure* consisting of *id*, *ego* and *superego*, *unconscious motives* and *defense mechanisms*. However, Anna Freud and Erikson emphasize ego development, and Winnicott and Kohut, the development of the *self*. Psychodynamic theories are concerned with the child's relationships with other people, often seen in the form of *object relations*. Emde, Stern and Fonagy have integrated general infant psychology with psychoanalytical theory.

4 *Behaviorism* emphasizes the role of learning in development, but also that humans are different from other species. An important element of *cognitive learning theory* is that people are conscious and goal-oriented agents in their own life. It integrates cognitive processes, individual beliefs and assumptions about the self and the world but builds on the idea that development is a cumulative learning process and that learning is the basis for most of the individual differences between children.

5 In *logical constructivism*, the child's perception of the world is constructed by the organism, and cognitive development is thought to follow logical principles. Children perceive the world qualitatively differently from adults, actively seek knowledge and go

through a long-lasting developmental process before they have acquired adult understanding and thinking. *Neo-Piagetians* such as Pascual-Leone, Case, Halford and Fischer share Piaget's constructivist basis, build on his ideas and integrate them with elements from other theories, notably information processing. Kohlberg extends Piaget's theory on moral development. Piaget's *new theory* takes earlier criticisms into account and is less based on logic.

6 According to *social constructivist theory*, children's cognition is shaped through interaction with others and through *internalization* of the mental tools of the culture. Children are guided into the activities and using the strategies and mental tools of their culture, first together with others, then on their own. *Neo-Vygotskians* have made innovative changes and revisions and elaborated Vygotsky's ideas in *activity theory*.

7 *Nativism* assumes that important aspects of human development are constrained by the genetic endowment, and that experience has limited influence on many aspects of development. The main argument is that children's experiences alone are insufficient for adapting to the world, and their own mind has to contribute from the start. According to *evolutionary psychologists*, development of aggression, altruism and morality must be understood in terms of their significance for survival in evolution. Bowlby's *ethological* theory of *attachment* has strongly influenced the understanding of children's early relations and has been important for clinical psychology, social work with children and raising children in general.

8 Bronfenbrenner's *bio-ecological* theory comprises *the proximal processes*, with interactions between children and the people around them and also meaningful objects or symbols. *The person* encompasses the individual's biological, cognitive, emotional and behavioral characteristics. *The context* consists of four systems: the *micro-*, *meso-*, *exo-* and *macrosystems*. *Time* encompasses the developmental time of the individual, as well as family time, historical time and so on.

9 *Information processing* models explain mental phenomena as information processed in one or several systems. Developmental change can be due to increases in processing speed or capacity and knowledge, and the use of new strategies. Information processing models have particularly influenced cognitive developmental

psychology, but also social development and the development of emotions, personality and behavior disorders.

10 *Critical developmental psychology* or *childhood psychology* maintains that assumptions about developmental regularities in children's internal processes should be replaced by analysis of the cultural practices. The course of development does not depend on any biological givens, but on the child's social and cultural setting. Cultural narratives define childhood, who the child is and the reasons why, and her position in society. When social and cultural changes alter widely held views about children, earlier knowledge about them is invalidated and has to be rewritten.

11 Theories about developmental psychology differ markedly in their ways of describing and explaining what children are capable of, can perceive, feel, think and do at different ages. This reflects children's very varied capacities and the complexity of the developmental process. It can be difficult to establish which of the contradictory theories may be correct, but the truth is not likely to be found somewhere halfway between two perspectives. If a theoretical assumption is shown to be correct, a contradictory assumption must be wrong.

Core Issues

*   The concepts that are needed for explaining human development in general and individual differences.
*   The status of different theoretical models for understanding child and adolescent development.

Suggestions for Further Reading

Beilin, H. (1992). Piaget's new theory. In H. Beilin & P. B. Pufall (Eds), *Piaget's theory: Prospects and possibilities* (pp. 1–17). Hillsdale, NJ: Lawrence Erlbaum.

Bowlby, J. (1982). Attachment and loss: Retrospect and prospect. *American Journal of Orthopsychiatry, 52*, 664–678.

Burman, E. (2001). Beyond the baby and the bathwater: Postdualistic developmental psychologies for diverse childhoods. *European Early Childhood Education Research Journal, 9*, 5–22.

Geary, D. C., & Bjorklund, D. F. (2000). Evolutionary developmental psychology. *Child Development, 71*, 57–65.

Gilmore, K. (2008). Psychoanalytic developmental theory: A contemporary reconsideration. *Journal of the American Psychoanalytic Association, 56*, 885–907.

Karpov, Y. V. (2005). *The neo-Vygotskian approach to child development.* Cambridge: Cambridge University Press.

Martí, E., & Rodríguez, C. (Eds) (2012). *After Piaget.* New Brunswick, NJ: Transaction Publishers.

Yermolayeva, Y., & Rakison, D. H. (2014). Connectionist modeling of developmental changes in infancy: Approaches, challenges, and contributions. *Psychological Bulletin, 140*, 224–355.

Part III

Methods of Gaining Knowledge about Children

21

Observations

Both researchers and practitioners use systematic methods to collect information about children. Researchers investigate children's typical and atypical development, the presence of variation and how particular characteristics of children and the environment contribute to different developmental trajectories, using a variety of methods. Some map the development of traits and how they relate to each other in the general child **population**, others compare children who have different variants of the same gene or grow up under different environmental conditions, while others again describe the developmental course of individual children. The choice of method is closely related to the study's theoretical or practical basis and what it intends to examine (Lerner et al., 2009). Theory and purpose thus act as "filters" that allow certain types of data to pass through and block out others. For practitioners, it is the child's possible problems or disorders that guide the collection of information.

Research is often about how children and adolescents act in a particular situation, for example when they are exposed to adult anger and aggression (see Book 6, *Emotions, Temperament, Personality, Moral, Prosocial and Antisocial Development*, Chapter 9). This requires some kind of observation and a registration of the activities and behavior of one or more individuals. The observer may for instance see, hear or record what children say and do when they are playing, talking, arguing and so on.

The observer may participate in the activity being observed, give instructions or simply observe, sometimes by using one or several video cameras. All observations involve *selection* and *interpretation*, and the adoption of one perspective where several are possible. Something

DOI: 10.4324/9781003291275-24

is always left out. A good observer is aware of his or her own interests, perspectives and other factors that can lead to bias in the collection of information or unequal treatment of observations.

In planning an observation, it is common to prepare categories that define and specify the things to be observed. Such categories may describe where children are located (in the sand box, on the swing, at the dining table), how they move (crawling, walking, running), what they are looking at (father, another child, a toy), what they are playing with (a car, a toy block, a ball) or the feelings they express (joy, anger, sadness) (see Table 21.1). The categories in each area should be unambiguous and mutually exclusive.

Naturalistic observations take place in the everyday environment where children usually spend their time, without influence by the observer. They may include observations of how children play and communicate with other children and adults, how they orient themselves in traffic or how they use their mobile phones. Box 21.1 describes a study that compares how children play at home with their mothers and fathers.

Many of the earliest studies were *diary studies* in which the researchers (who were also the children's parents) wrote down what their children said or did in diary form (Bühler, 1928; Darwin, 1877; Stern, 1912). Piaget presents many systematic observations of his own children in his early books (e.g., Piaget, 1950, 1952). In the field of

Table 21.1 Common dimensions in the description of observations (based on Robson, 2002)

1	Space	Design of the physical environment, rooms, outside spaces and so on
2	Persons	Names and relevant details of the persons included in the observations
3	Activities	The various activities in which the observed individuals participate
4	Objects	Physical elements, objects, furniture and so on
5	Actions	Specific actions performed by each person
6	Events	Special events, such as gatherings and meetings
7	Time	Sequence of events
8	Goal	What the individuals being observed try to achieve
9	Emotions	Emotions shown or described by the individuals in particular contexts

Box 21.1 Children's Play with Mothers and Fathers (John et al., 2013)

Interested families were recruited from two centers for preschool-aged children. The home visits started by informing families of their rights as a participant and obtaining their consent. All observations began with a child–mother observation, which lasted for approximately 18–20 minutes, followed by child–father observation, which lasted for approximately 12–15 minutes, and took place at either the dining table or a play table in the living room. Both the child–mother and the child–father dyads chose from a set of toys comprising play dough and molds, building blocks, coloring book and markers, and a storybook. During the observation, only the participating dyad and the observer remained in the room. All observations were videotaped for subsequent analysis, and each family received $75 for their participation. The researchers categorized each of the activities of the child–parent dyads and rated parental sensitivity, structuring, non-intrusiveness and non-hostility, and child responsiveness and involvement, on a scale from low (1) to high (7). The analyses of the observations showed that the mothers tended to structure the children's play, "teach" them, guide their behavior and engage them in empathic conversations. The interactions with fathers included more physical play and child-led interactions, and the fathers tended to motivate and challenge the children and behave more like age mates. However, the average emotional availability was not significantly different. With this methodology the researchers showed that young children have different interaction patterns in play with their mothers and fathers.

language development, it is still common for researchers to study their own children, as this type of study requires close monitoring (Carpendale & Carpendale, 2010; Dromi, 1993; Tomasello, 1992).

Experiments

Experiments are often used when something is difficult to observe in ordinary situations. Investigations of causal relations for example in young children's memory for events may require systematic observation under controlled conditions (see Book 4, *Cognition, Intelligence and Learning*, Part II). Here, "control" means that as many conditions as possible are kept constant so that the results are likely to reflect the factors that are targeted in the study. Factors that are not part of the experiment should ideally not affect the outcome. All subjects should be observed in the same way and treated equally, except when differential treatment is part of the experiment, such as in the experiment where two groups of children received different information about toys (Book 6, *Emotions, Temperament, Personality, Moral, Prosocial and Antisocial Development*), or when one group of children receives training, and another group does not.

Laboratory experiments are observations in customized environments and situations. One example is the "**Strange Situation**" which is used to elicit attachment behavior (see Book 7, *Social Relations, Self-awareness and Identity*, Chapter 4). The child is first separated from and then reunited with a caregiver, following a carefully planned procedure and using clearly defined categories for the child's behavior. One potential pitfall of laboratory studies that explore an otherwise naturally occurring situation is low **ecological validity**, because children may behave differently in unfamiliar surroundings. Many developmental experiments, however, do not aim to recreate a natural environment, but to test theoretical assumptions about how children act and react under very specific conditions. Robert Fantz's (1958) classic experiments provided new and pioneering knowledge about the visual acuity of infants and their focus of attention, and thereby also about the bases of cognitive and social development. Infants were shown visual patterns of varying complexity without any other distracting stimulation, a situation that differs considerably from infants' normal visual environment. Despite all the informal observations of thousands of generations of parents and other adults, infant vision had been greatly underestimated until this point. The abilities of infants would hardly have been uncovered so convincingly without an experimental laboratory method (see Book 3, *Perceptual and Motor Development*, Chapter 3).

Field experiments combine naturalistic observation and experimental control by studying the consequences of a systematic change in a natural environment for child and adult behavior. One example is a study that demonstrated the *Rosenthal effect*. Teachers were told that some of the students in their class were expected to do well in school on the basis of their scores on intelligence tests, but the students' scores were actually drawn at random. The experiment showed that the false information had a bearing on both the teachers' assessment and the students' performance at school: those who were expected to do better on the basis of fake test results did in fact perform better in school (see Book 4, *Cognition, Intelligence and Learning*, Chapter 28).

Some Common Problems in Observing Children

Many factors can influence observations of children. The presence of an adult observer will always affect them. Children may be shy or have trouble understanding verbal instructions in an unfamiliar setting. In a study of the language of 4-year-olds, several children reacted to being alone with an unfamiliar adult by answering almost exclusively in monosyllables, while the parents reported that their children usually spoke in sentences (Fintoft et al., 1983). Moreover, adults represent power and knowledge, and it is particularly difficult to observe children's spontaneous interactions without influencing them too much. Even adults behave slightly differently toward children when they are observed by an experimenter or recorded on video.

There is no simple formula for overcoming the problems that may arise in connection with observing children. Instead, it is a matter of being aware of potential problems, trying to reduce their impact and taking into account the uncertainty they create in drawing observation-based conclusions.

22

Questionnaires and Interviews

Sometimes researchers need to investigate a large number of children and adolescents to be sure that the information can be generalized to all boys and girls of that age, for example how many are exposed to bullying and how they react when they see other students being bullied in school (see Book 6, *Emotions, Temperament, Personality, Moral, Prosocial and Antisocial Development*, Chapter 27). It would be difficult to observe enough children and adolescents involved in bullying, and it would take a lot of time and resources. It is more efficient to collect the information by interviewing the children themselves or their parents, or asking them to complete questionnaires (e.g., Baldry, 2003; Fekkes et al., 2005).

Questionnaires usually consist of close-ended questions with multiple-choice answers to be marked by the child or an adult, for example by indicating on a scale from 1 (never) to 5 (always) whether they see "Kids who hit or push others" (Pfeiffer & Pinquart, 2014). The advantage of questionnaires is that it is relatively easy to collect a large number of answers, sometimes with the help of the Internet (Gosling & Mason, 2015). The disadvantage is that the number of questions and alternative answers is limited and allows little insight into the reasoning behind the answers, even if informants can add comments.

Interviews are conversations between an interviewer and an interviewee, based on an interview guide. They can be as structured as a questionnaire, but are usually *semi-structured*, with room for clarifying questions and clearing up of potential misunderstandings. Although they are more time-consuming, the interviewer can collect more detailed information, respond with follow-up questions and get deeper insight into the interviewee's thoughts and feelings. This is particularly important in interviewing children, who often interpret

DOI: 10.4324/9781003291275-25

questions from their own point of view (Eder & Fingerson, 2001). Interviews are not commonly used in the study of younger children because they can have difficulty communicating their thoughts and ideas verbally, but are widely used in studies of older children and adolescents and to gather information from parents, teachers and other adults. Interviews with children are important because they may give a quite different picture than information from their parents or teachers (Davies & Wright, 2008; Madge & Fassam, 1982), but they require sensitivity, ability to listen and good communication skills.

Archival Research

Many public institutions collect and store information routinely, and this material can to some extent be obtained, analyzed and interpreted (Scott & Attia, 2017). Public records with information about the population are available in most modern societies. Some are widely accessible in the form of a large amount of statistical material that makes it impossible to identify individuals, and analysis may give insight into the influences of different caregiving environments. Box 23.1 is an example of a study based on archival data. Other records have strict limitations on who can access them and how they can be used owing to privacy protection laws. However, analysis of medical records or reports from health centers, hospitals, kindergartens, schools and school psychologists may give important information about the effect of different intervention measures. Archives represent an efficient and time-effective way of accessing information, but their drawback is that researchers cannot influence the information or ask follow-up questions.

Box 23.1   Parental Demographics and Children's Socioeconomic Achievements (Erola et al., 2016)

The researchers analyzed public data provided by Statistics Finland on the occupational position of 29,282 children and on the parents' education, occupational class and income when the children were 0–4, 5–9, 10–14, 15–19, 20–24 and 25–29 years old. They found that **socioeconomic status** in young adulthood was significantly related to parental education but not to parental income and social class. A large prospective study for investigating these kinds of relationships would have taken much time and resources.

DOI: 10.4324/9781003291275-26

Methodologies

Studies of children differ from one another along several dimensions: there are qualitative and quantitative studies, group and case studies, **retrospective** and **prospective studies**, and **cross-sectional** and **longitudinal studies**.

Quantitative and Qualitative Methods

Quantitative and qualitative methodologies are the two main classes of research methodologies. Quantitative methods are used when the phenomena in question can be counted or measured in other ways and are often based on questions such as *who, where, when, what* and *how many*. For example, one can register the age at which a sample of children speak their first word, count how many words the children use at the age of 2 and calculate the average age and typical age range for the first word, the average number of words and the minimum and maximum number of words at 2 years, and the children's **mean length of utterance** (Brown, 1973). Based on these data, statistical relationships (correlations) can be established between the age at which the children spoke their first word and the size of their vocabulary and mean length of utterance at the age of 2 years. Statistics can be used to calculate whether there is more than a random difference in vocabulary among children from different social backgrounds or among the younger and older siblings in a family.

Qualitative methods are often used to describe processes, with research questions such as *how* and *why* something happens. Events are described with words, and analyses typically involve text rather than numbers. By performing qualitative analyses of children's and adults' contributions in early conversations, for example, one can study how children learn sentences (Scollon, 1976; Tomasello, 1992).

DOI: 10.4324/9781003291275-27

Both quantitative and qualitative methods are rooted in a scientific argument that makes a case for a given phenomenon to be worthwhile and viable for study. If the research questions are best answered by measurable results, a quantitative approach is indicated. If they are best answered by descriptions of processes that are difficult to quantify and measure, a qualitative approach is preferable. *Mixed methods* can often provide more information and a broader perspective than one of the methodologies alone (Nelson, 2015; Tolan & Deutsch, 2015). Experimental data are usually, but not necessarily, quantitative. The same applies to studies based on questionnaires, which are often analyzed using statistics. Tests and other assessment instruments are designed to rank children and quantify the differences between them. Observations and interviews of children can be analyzed quantitatively as well as qualitatively, for example by tallying children's emotional statements as well as performing qualitative analyses that can shed light on their emotional involvement in a given situation (Lund, 2005; Yoshikawa et al., 2008). Thus, the lines between the two approaches are not always clear, and sometimes both methods are applied to the same observational data, such as in a study that surveyed parents and preschool teachers on when children should start in kindergarten (Undheim & Drugli, 2012). *Microgenetic* studies, which include both observations and conversations over time, are used to gain insight into how children think and solve problems (Siegler, 2006). Observations of **quantitative changes** in the occurrence of different child actions may direct the microgenetic "microscope" at processes in the transitional phases for a qualitative analysis of where the changes seem to occur, for example the point in development where children begin to express understanding of mind and false belief (Flynn et al., 2007).

Group and Case Studies

Many researchers are interested in the emergence and developmental consequences of specific traits, such as **sociability** or shyness (see Rubin & Coplan, 2010), and such studies may require a relatively large number of children. In order to investigate the relationship between shyness and social development, it is necessary to compare shy children with a group of children who are not shy and at the same time do not differ in other ways. If the groups differed in other areas, for example in relative numbers of boys and girls, any differences in social development could just as well be due to these factors as to the difference in shyness.

In some studies, one of the groups is treated or influenced in a specific way and compared with a group that has not been exposed to the same treatment or influence. One study, for example, found that a cod liver oil supplement had a positive effect on the cognitive development of infants (Helland et al., 2003). The "**experimental group**" received the supplement, while a similar substance was given to the "**control group**," a placebo. The control group corresponds to the experimental group in every other way, but "controls" the effect of the supplement by not receiving it. The children in this group had the same average birth weight and social background, and none of the parents were told whether their child received the supplement or the placebo until after the study was finished. Only then could Helland be sure that the supplement made a difference.

Today, there is a general demand that educational and clinical practice should be evidence-based, that choice of assessment and intervention measures should be based on knowledge about documented effects and solid research (Berninger, 2015; Stoiber et al., 2016). This demand has partly emerged from the early disagreements between different theoretical approaches in child mental health and between psychodynamic treatment and behavioral and cognitive treatment, and it has contributed to a wider use of interventions with documented effect (Forte et al., 2014). Clinical studies with a high degree of control, where similar subjects are randomly allocated to a treatment or non-treatment group, are considered the highest level of evidence. However, comparing treatment and no treatment may not be a good basis for deciding the efficacy of an intervention, as most interventions are better than nothing. Decisions about intervention for children with severe disabilities, for example, should be based on thorough knowledge about relevant interventions. New interventions should be compared with interventions that are already in use, and studies should thus have an experimental treatment group and a treatment-as-usual group (e.g., von Tetzchner et al., 2013).

Individual children can show a variation in development not otherwise found in the group. Descriptions of individual developmental trajectories can therefore supplement knowledge of development based on group studies (von Eye et al., 2015). Studies of individual children who show unusual abilities such as musicality or arithmetic skills can furthermore contribute knowledge about how these abilities develop in relation to other developmental areas. In a similar way, it can be useful to study children who are blind or deaf or have neuro-developmental disorders. Clinical descriptions of individual children are called *case studies*. One advantage of such studies is that they can go into greater depth and provide insight into the processes underlying the atypical development, also in a scientific sense. Their downside is that the findings can be difficult to generalize and apply to children in other contexts. Case studies typically include both qualitative and quantitative information, but most of the data tend to be qualitative. Case studies are of great importance to clinical developmental psychology (see Parker & Hagan-Burke, 2007; Yin, 2009).

Cross-sectional and Longitudinal Studies

There are two ways of obtaining information about the general development trajectory of a given characteristic in children. *Cross-sectional studies* try to map the development process by comparing children at different age levels (see Figure 24.1), for example by observing the children's aggressive actions in typical situations or letting parents complete questionnaires about their children's behavior and background. Studies show that young children show a higher frequency of hitting than older children and positive relations between the number of aggressive actions and various environmental factors, such as family relations, time with violent computer games and so on (see Book 6, *Emotions, Temperament, Personality, Moral, Prosocial and Antisocial Development*, Chapter 28, and Book 7, *Social Relations, Self-awareness and Identity*, Chapter 38). The advantage of cross-sectional studies is that they are time-efficient. Researchers avoid having to wait for children to grow up, and children are spared some of the strain as they are studied at only a single age level.

Cross-sectional studies can show what is typical for children at different age levels but reveal little about the actual course of development. If one has observed aggressive actions in 2-, 6- and 10-year-olds, it is impossible to know whether the same or different children exhibit most aggressive behaviors at these ages, whether their aggression is stable over time, or whether there is a relationship between their early characteristics, experiences and environment and their later aggressive behavior. This requires a longitudinal study in which the same children are observed at the ages of 2, 6 and 10 years. This approach would provide more insight into the developmental process and the

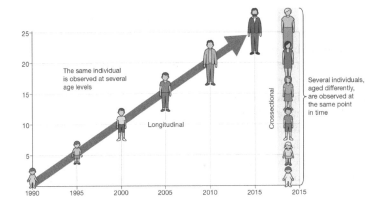

Figure 24.1 Longitudinal and cross-sectional studies.

Longitudinal studies examine the same individuals at different points in their lives. Here, the participants were observed at birth in 1990, and in 1995, 2000, 2005, 2010 and 2015. Cross-sectional studies examine a number of differently aged individuals at the same time. Here, the participants were newborns and 5, 10, 15, 20 and 25 years old in 2015.

developmental courses of children with different characteristics and experiences, their vulnerability and resilience. Relatively short-term longitudinal studies are common (a search with "longitudinal" in Google Scholar creates over 4 million hits), and several longitudinal studies have lasted for 30 years and longer (for example, Bergman et al., 2014; Block & Block, 2006; Caspi et al., 2016; Sroufe et al., 2010). In 1939, Sol Seim (1997) launched a unique longitudinal study that began when the participants were 13 years old and continued until they were nearly 70 in 1994. Seim herself was over 80 years old at the time. Of the 100 original 13-year-olds, 49 were still part of the study when they turned 70.

Since longitudinal studies are very time-consuming, studies conducted over many years are relatively rare, but they are absolutely essential. Without such studies, there would be no basis for a developmental psychology based on scientific evidence (Campos et al., 2008; Kagan, 2008b).

Prospective and Retrospective Studies

When researchers follow one or several children over time, typically using observations, questionnaires and interviews, this is a *prospective study*. **Retrospective studies** are based on information about passed events, such as children's earlier development and experiences. The source of information is usually parents and others who know the children well, but the information is often colored by the passage of time and therefore somewhat unreliable, especially when events and recollections go far back in time. In this case, archival information can provide a supplement to the information contributed by parents. For example, the diaries of family members and private videos have been used to document the development of children with autism spectrum disorder *before* they received the diagnosis (Zwaigenbaum et al., 2007).

Even though they are to a certain extent unreliable, retrospective studies are important. It can be difficult for example to map the development of children with a rare disorder before the disorder is detected. If one were to follow children with a rare disorder prospectively, from before the disorder makes its appearance, one would need to observe a group of children large enough to be likely to include children with the disorder in question. This would imply observing many children whose development is unrelated to the focus of study. The Norwegian Mother and Child Cohort Study (Magnus et al., 2016), which involves over 100,000 parents and children and includes regular information on the course of pregnancy and childhood, is an example of a prospective study large enough to incorporate information about the development of children with rare conditions.

Cross-cultural Studies

Every child grows up in a society with certain values, norms, activities and ways of organizing and doing things, and styles and methods of parenting vary considerably between countries (Selin, 2014). Society is an important part of the childhood environment and impacts most developmental areas (see Bornstein, 2010). Comparing children growing up in different cultures is a way of studying the impact of both biological and cultural factors and can yield information about the types of environmental factors necessary and adequate for normal development. The characteristics of **child–directed speech**, for example, are considered to be important for language development (see Book 5, *Communication and Language Development*, Chapter 8), but are not equally prominent in all cultures (Schaffer, 1989). Also, how parents play with their children varies considerably between countries (Roopnarine & Davidson, 2015).

A consequence of such cultural differences is that the results of studies in one culture are not always transferable to other cultures. This is an important argument for studying children who grow up in different cultures. Asian and North American parents for example respond differently to the emotional expressions of their children (see Book 6, *Emotions, Temperament, Personality, Moral, Prosocial and Antisocial Development*, Chapter 4). On the basis of either American or Chinese studies alone, an understanding of how children develop emotional regulation would be highly biased. In a similar vein, Robert Sternberg maintains that the study of culture is "necessary, not just nice," and that "developmental psychologists can do a better job of understanding and leveraging the strengths of people from diverse environmental contexts if those strengths are viewed in a cultural framework" (2014, p. 209).

25

Special Methods for Studying Infants

Children's understanding of the world emerges gradually, and how infants perceive their environment is of great interest to developmental research but challenging from a methodological point of view. As infants cannot directly communicate what they see or hear or solve tasks involving complex verbal or non-verbal instructions, research methods are based on habituation and conditioning, visual exploration and physiological and neurophysiological measurements. Habituation and conditioning are also used in fetal research (see Book 2, *Genes, Fetal Development and Early Neurological Development*, Part II).

Habituation and Dishabituation

Infants explore the world and are generally interested in what happens around them. They are typically attentive to new things and events but, when they are repeatedly shown the same object or get to hear the same sound, they will gradually react less and less, and eventually stop responding altogether. They "lose" attention, or *habituate*. When children discover something new, they will respond more strongly once again, or *dishabituate*. **Dishabituation** thus requires the child to be able to distinguish between the original stimulation and the new one. This has been methodically exploited by researchers to discover the types of stimulation, situations and events infants are able to differentiate, such as their ability to distinguish between speech sounds (see Book 5, *Communication and Language Development*, Chapter 6).

DOI: 10.4324/9781003291275-28

Conditioning

Studies of infants make use of both classical and operant conditioning (see Book 4, *Cognition, Intelligence and* Learning, Chapter 35). An example of **classical conditioning** is a study in which a tone was played to infants right before a puff of air was blown onto their eyes and automatically caused them to blink. After several presentations, the children blinked when they heard the tone, "preparing" for the air they had learned would follow (Little et al., 1984). An example of **operant conditioning** is a study in which 3-month-olds learned to move a leg to activate a mobile hanging above the bed (Rovee-Collier & Cuevas, 2009a; see Book 4, *Cognition, Intelligence and Learning*, Chapter 10).

Visual Exploration

Attention is selective, and children's attention therefore gives information about what is and is not of interest to them. Head-mounted cameras and equipment that records where infants look, pupil dilation and eye blink have become important tools for studying how they explore and perceive their environment and react to events in the visual world (Eckstein et al., 2017; Gredebäck et al., 2010; Yoshida & Smith, 2008).

Visual Preference

When infants are shown two pictures or objects, they often look longer at one of them than the other, and generally this is not a matter of chance. This tendency to look longer at one visual stimulus than another, also known as *preferential looking*, is used among other things to map the vision, memory and concepts of infants (Golinkoff et al., 2013). Fantz (1961) uses the preferential looking method to determine the types of stimulation most "interesting" to newborns, that is, what they look at the longest (see Book 3, *Perceptual and Motor Development*, Chapter 3).

Other studies build on the assumption that children will look longest at the picture or object that represents something new (**novelty preference**). When 3- to 4-month-olds are shown two pictures of a face with the same emotional expression, followed by the same picture together with a picture of a new facial expression, the infants will look longest at the new expression (provided they have had enough time to familiarize themselves with the first facial expression). Novelty preference shows that children remember the first facial expression and are able to see that it differs from the new facial expression (Fagan & Detterman, 1992).

Some studies are based on the assumption that unexpected phenomena have greater attention value than ordinary ones (e.g., Onishi & Baillargeon, 2005). Studies have found that infants look longer at a seemingly impossible event, such as a toy block hanging in the air without support, than they do in an otherwise identical situation in which the block is supported by a surface (Baillargeon et al., 1995; see Book 4, Chapter 13). The results have been interpreted to mean that, even at this age, infants have some understanding of physical forces and that toy blocks cannot float freely in the air (Baillargeon et al., 2009).

Physiological Reactions

Children's physiological responses can also provide information on how they perceive what happens in their surroundings. For instance, infants react to novelty with a decrease in heart rate (**orienting response**). Loud noises and other forms of aversive stimulation lead to an increase in heart rate (Richards, 2001; Rovee-Collier & Barr, 2001). **Cortisol** levels are often used as a measure of stress, but the production of cortisol is also affected by factors unrelated to stress (Reznick, 2013).

Neurophysiological Measures

The methods for exploring brain functions are constantly improving (see Book 2, *Genes, Fetal Development and Early Neurological Development*, Chapter 12) and open up new ways of studying infants. Just like dishabituation, the *mismatch response* (see Book 2, *Genes, Fetal Development and Early Neurological Development*, Chapter 12) is used to determine when a child perceives something novel. One advantage of this method is that it requires no cooperation on the part of the child, who can be asleep during the procedure.

The Methods Are Important but Difficult to Interpret

The methods are important for obtaining an empirical basis for theories about infant cognition. However, a narrow repertoire of reactions is used to measure a broad range of hypothetical cognitive functions, including concept formation and reasoning about social and physical phenomena. Preferential looking in particular is frequently used (Baillargeon, 1987; Dahl et al., 2013; Fantz, 1956), but what children look at and how long they look at different things and events are affected by many factors and change considerably throughout infancy (and later). Many interpretations of findings are controversial, and several researchers argue that far more knowledge and understanding are often ascribed to infants than warranted by the studies (Aslin, 2007; Bishop, 2007; Tafreshi et al., 2014). In an analysis of methods and conclusions, Kagan (2008a) points out that the results of infant studies commonly allow for widely differing interpretations, and that many of the studies lack observations that could corroborate the researchers' interpretations of the infants' preferential looking patterns.

26

Criteria for Research Methodology

Sound research methodology has to fill a number of special requirements to ensure that the results can be trusted, including transparency, representativeness, reliability and validity. These requirements are met in somewhat different ways, depending on whether they have to do with quantitative or qualitative methods.

Transparency means that all the details of the method are openly available. The main requirement of quantitative research is **replicability**, where the method is explained so clearly and unambiguously that another researcher can carry out an identical study and examine whether the outcome can be reproduced or was caused by accidental circumstances. Such replications are a necessary part of research, since the results of many frequently cited studies have shown themselves to be non-replicable, and therefore invalid (Asendorpf et al., 2013; Stroebe et al., 2012). However, when replications fail, this does not necessarily mean that all the results of the original study were wrong, but points to the need for further theoretical and empirical work (Reese, 1999; Stroebe, 2016). Replications are thus not only a control mechanism to decide whether a study's results were valid, but an important basis for driving science.

In qualitative research, transparency is quite different. The observer should make his or her subjective standpoint clear, including perceptions, opinions and attitudes, and give a sufficiently "thick" description that allows other researchers to understand the findings and confirm that the conclusions are reasonable (Biggerstaff, 2012). A researcher may have personal experiences or qualifications that could be of significance to the study and therefore need reflection, but it is mainly the researcher's theoretical perspective that needs to be clarified, rather than his or her personal background. Piaget never discussed his

DOI: 10.4324/9781003291275-29

own background but always elucidated the theoretical assumptions behind the questions he asked children when applying his qualitative **"clinical method"** to find out how children reason in their problem solving (see Book 4, *Cognition, Intelligence and Learning*, Chapter 3).

Research not only is generally interested in the particular children being studied, but wishes to say something about the group or groups to which the children belong, for example the **prevalence** of language disorders in 4–5-year-olds (Harrison & McLeod, 2010). Therefore it is essential for the *sample* of children to be *representative* of the *population* they are part of. A population consists of all the children for whom the study results are intended to be valid. Depending on the population one wants to study, a **representative sample** may involve an equal number of girls and boys, an equal number of children from every age level, different social classes and so on. If a study aims at investigating characteristics typical of girls, it is not enough to study girls. If the researcher's hypothesis for instance is that girls have better language skills than boys, the language of both boys and girls has to be studied (Leaper & Smith, 2004).

Qualitative research does not require the outcome to be quantitatively representative, meaning that the subjects of the study need not be representative of a larger group. However, observations must be considered adequate and typical enough by the researcher to be the target of research with validity beyond itself. Qualitative analyses of interviews with adolescents who have mobility impairments for example are usually designed not to say something about that particular group of adolescents, but to provide a more general insight into the living conditions of adolescents who grow up with mobility impairments (see Madge & Fassam, 1982; Wickenden, 2011). The observations must therefore be representative of the experiences of this group.

Reliability

A study may include many observations and several observers, and, for the observations to be reliable, the observational categories and measurement methods used should yield the same result with all observers and with repeated observations. A common method of testing **reliability** is to let several observers rate the same situation or video recording independently of one another, based on a specific set of observational categories (**inter-observer reliability**). If one observer claims to have seen a child smile five times, and another observer has seen ten smiles in the same space of time, they clearly use different criteria for what they consider to be a smile. This leads to unreliable results, as the observers are not using the same categories. To meet the requirements of reliability, they must agree in advance on a common set of criteria, the only way of ensuring that measurements are consistent and comparable. This is not to say that observers are always entirely certain of the **emotion** shown by a child, but mutual uncertainty about a child's particular expression is also an indication of reliability.

Qualitative methods, too, require observations that are accurate enough to be trustworthy. Video and sound recordings must contain all relevant and necessary information. Observational notes must be sufficiently systematic and extensive, follow accepted standards, be written during or shortly after the observation and be accessible to third parties (Wolcott, 1994).

Validity

Validity concerns whether the method measures what it is supposed to measure and the results can provide answers to the questions posed by the study (Boorsboom et al., 2004). Reliability is necessary but not sufficient for establishing validity. A method is of little use if it is reliable but does not measure what the study is about. Although children's height can be measured with great accuracy, height will never be a valid measure of intelligence. The question of validity is equally central to quantitative and qualitative research.

There are several types of validity. *Construct validity* is the degree to which something that is observed or measured is a true representation of what the study intends or claims to measure, for example that children's answers on a questionnaire about their routines at home match the observations of what they actually do at home. *Predictive validity* is the ability to foresee the future, where measurements made at one point can predict later characteristics or performance. This type of validity is especially important for the use of tests and other assessment instruments. When Binet and Simon (1905) designed the first intelligence test, the aim was to find children who would need special help in school. For a test to be valid, children who have higher scores should do better in school than children who receive lower scores. Also today school psychologists try to find school starters who may need special help and they thus depend on tests that can give a valid assessment. If an assessment is not valid, it serves no purpose either.

Construct validity is central to developmental psychology as it concerns the way in which development in different areas is measured and described – the particular observations that form the basis for conclusions about the mechanisms involved in development.

Internal validity describes the soundness of assumptions about causal relationships after finding some type of relation between two variables, for example between measures of **working memory** and reading (Cozby, 1993). There are many "threats" to internal validity that may lead to wrong conclusions. These can be coincidences, such as when the school bully drops out of school at the same time as the school takes action against bullying. It looks as if the school's initiative had an effect, whereas the decrease in bullying is actually due to the fact that the student who did the bullying is no longer in school. An evaluation of a program supposed to promote social development has to take into consideration that children continually develop and include observations of social development in a control group of children who do not attend the program. Without a control group, children's ordinary development during program attendance can mistakenly be ascribed to the program. And apparent changes in children's behavior can be due to the use of different routines or observational categories at different points in time (Cook & Campbell, 1979).

External validity concerns the extent to which information can be generalized – whether the same behavior or characteristics found in the study subjects will also be found in others. Non-representative samples, observations made under special circumstances and unique historical contexts can easily jeopardize external validity. A study of **gross motor skills** based on children's skiing abilities may have a high degree of validity in Nordic countries but cannot be generalized to children living closer to the equator.

The concept of validity is less clear in qualitative research (Creswell & Miller, 2000). Zambo (2004) includes establishing credibility (stability and plausibility of data), transferability (applicability to other situations), dependability (trustworthiness of the data) and confirmability (that the data are in accordance with other observations). In a study on the impact of **dyslexia** on school life, she tried to ensure validity by making observations over a long time period, conducting interviews with students and teachers, making field notes and journal entries, reflecting on her own theoretical perspective and potential biases, using "triangulation" (comparing results from different methods) and asking participants if they agreed with the descriptions and interpretations.

27

Assessment

The function of clinical assessment of children is usually to gather information on how they understand, think, feel and act, and on the characteristics of their physical and social environment, especially the quality of their relations within the family and with children and adults outside the family. The assessment is usually initiated on the basis of a concern and a referral, and these will guide the assessment. The goal is to examine whether the child has any disorders or difficulties in areas requiring treatment, special education or other measures, or whether changes need to be made in the child's environment. In a clinical context, assessment is nearly always individual, but the use of tests and other assessment instruments is common in research studies of both typical and atypical development.

Conversations and Interviews

Most assessments of children begin with an anamnestic interview, a conversation with the parents about the child's developmental history and the observations that led to the referral. This may include structured and standardized interviews about the child's functioning in specific areas. These conversations provide information about the child and the family, but also help professionals and parents get to know each other and establish an *alliance*, a shared understanding of the child's strengths and weaknesses and the types of measures that may be necessary. When possible, older children and adolescents should take part in the conversations and interviews and be included in the alliance.

DOI: 10.4324/9781003291275-30

Observations

Observations at home, in kindergarten and at school can give the practitioner an impression for instance of the child's skills, play, working effort, attention and social functioning. It can be useful to observe the child in both structured and unstructured situations, together with other children and with adults. For some areas, there are checklists with predesigned categories that make it easier to record the child's actions, such as different types of play and activities (Barton, 2010; Kelly-Vance et al., 2002).

In some cases, it can be helpful to use video recordings to document how the child functions in different situations. The child may behave differently in school and at home with the parents, and parents may use video to document the child's home behavior. Children with selective mutism are able to speak but do not speak with people outside the family (Steinhausen et al., 2006; see Chapter 33, this volume). An audio recording with the parents may be useful to get an impression of the child's **expressive language**.

Tests

Tests are designed to rank children. They contain tasks standardized to measure individual performance in a specific area and under standard conditions. A large number of tests are available, embracing a wide range of skills and abilities (see Miller, 2007; Sattler, 2002). Tests of intelligence and specific cognitive skills are often part of assessment (see Book 4, *Cognition, Intelligence and Learning*, Part V), together with language testing (see Book 5, *Communication and language*, Chapter 12). Other tests include perceptual and motor skills (Book 3, *Perceptual and Motor Development*, Part I), attention and executive skills (Book 4, *Cognition, Intelligence and Learning*, Part II), social cognitive skills (Book 4, *Cognition, Intelligence and Learning*, Part IV) and emotional understanding (Book 6, *Emotions, Temperament, Personality, Moral, Prosocial and Antisocial Development*, Chapter 7).

It is important that tests be carried out according to the manual, and only by professionals with a license to use them. The instructions must be formulated so the child can understand them. This is often an issue in the assessment of immigrant children. If the child does not understand the instructions, the results will not reflect the child's ability to solve the tasks. In addition, the tasks must correspond to the child's level of competence. Tasks that are too easy or too difficult can be perceived as both boring and meaningless. The tester must maintain a pace adapted to the child and be sensitive to how the child experiences the test situation. The presentation of many difficult tasks should be followed by a break, even if highly motivated children might claim they do not need one.

Testing requires good communication. The tester must be thoroughly familiar with the test and so well prepared that there is no need to consult the manual or cause unnecessary delays during the test procedure. Before testing begins, it can be useful to inform the child about the test and the reasons for taking it, and ask whether the child has any questions. It is not unusual for children to have practical questions about how long the test will take, whether they will get a break and so on. The tester should also engage in a bit of small talk before the test begins and spend some time getting to know the child. However, there should be no small talk during the testing as this may take the child's attention away from the tasks.

Feedback has to focus on the child's *effort*. Ideally, the child should have a sense of doing well, even if the answers are wrong. Usually, it is enough to say something like "Good!" or "It's going very well." The tester must not tell the child whether the answer is right or wrong, except on trial tasks prescribed by the manual, as this would invalidate any future use of the test with the same child. Children can remember the answer even if they don't know why it is correct. Taking notes should also be done in such a way that the child cannot see whether the answer is right or wrong. The easiest way of doing this is to write down what the child says or does. It is important to get the child to focus on solving each task, not on whether the answer is correct.

Testing of Special Groups

All testing must be adapted to the individual child's abilities. Although tests are designed to be suitable for most children, it may still be necessary to adapt the test situation and the material being used. Children who are deaf and use sign language have to be given instructions in sign language. It is not always enough for a sign language interpreter to translate the instructions one by one. Translations of more complex instructions should be planned and prepared in advance (Reesman et al., 2014). Assessments of children with severe visual impairments often involve using the language part of the test alone. Tasks consisting of images with a missing item, categorization based on shape and colours, puzzles and checkerboard patterns are unsuitable for children with poor vision. However, there are tests with non-visual and non-verbal tasks for the assessment of children with visual impairments (Smith & Amato, 2012; Zebehazy et al., 2012).

Children with severe motor impairments cannot perform tasks requiring them to physically construct something or follow action instructions such as "put the doll on the chair," but some tests are adapted for computers with equipment for eye-tracking, and the child or adolescent can answer by looking at the right response alternative (Kurmanaviciute & Stadskleiv, 2017; Stadskleiv et al., 2017). Children with less severe motor impairments may be able to perform such actions, but often use so many cognitive resources on the physical execution itself that they score below what their ability to reason would suggest. The same applies to children with developmental motor coordination disorder or dyspraxia (see Chapter 31, this volume). For these groups, it may be necessary to use tests that require a minimum of motor skills, allot more time and make allowances for motor problems in interpreting their cognitive skills.

Any special arrangements and adjustments must be taken into account in the interpretation of test results. When testing takes place under specially tailored conditions, the **norms** merely provide a guideline as they are usually based on a representative group of children with typical development. Children with atypical development are rarely included in **norm-referenced tests**. Consequently, these norms do not apply to them and must be used with caution. However, the results can still be useful for optimizing the child's learning situation. Some children may benefit from a **dynamic assessment** as a supplement to regular testing (see below).

Checklists

Checklists have become a common element in assessment. They consist of questions about the child's skills, behavior and everyday functioning. They are usually completed by parents, teachers and other adults, but checklists can also be completed by older children and adolescents. In addition, checklists are used by professionals to structure their own observations. One example of this is an instrument for observing children's everyday language (Cordier et al., 2014). The *Vineland Adaptive Behavior Scale* (Sparrow et al., 2005) is used to map everyday skills, language, social-cognitive and social skills. The *Child Behavior Check List* (CBCL; Achenbach & Rescorla, 2000, 2001) assesses emotional and behavioral disorders. Other checklists measure temperament, life quality, characteristics of the environment and how parents and other people in the child's surroundings experience their situation.

Parents are an important source of information about the child, but should not be responsible for assessing their child's development. Their view of the child is colored by their own perspective as parents, and often there are considerable differences in how parents, professionals and the children themselves answer questions about the child's temperament, emotions and behavior (De Los Reyes & Kazdin, 2005; Rescorla et al., 2014; Seifer et al., 1994).

Many checklists are screening instruments designed to identify children who should be further assessed with regard to disorders in general (Macy, 2012). Others aim to identify a particular disorder, such as autism spectrum disorder. It is important to use checklists that have questions that address the child's problems at that age. M-CHAT, for example, does not work particularly well for 18-month-olds, but can be useful from the age of 2 years (Beuker et al., 2014; Stenberg et al., 2014).

Analysis and Interpretation

Completing the testing procedure and filling out checklists are only the first stage in the assessment process. The main task is to analyze the results, describe functional profiles and collate test results, observations and information from interviews and conversations. It is especially important to compare the child's strengths and weaknesses as they emerge in a structured test situation with the child's functioning in structured and unstructured activities at home, in kindergarten and at school. Test scores are influenced by many factors and should not be considered a measure of the child's inborn abilities. In many countries it is therefore usual to present not scores but rather a broad characterization of the child's achievements, such as "average," "below average," "in the upper part of the normal variation," "gifted" or "mild intellectual disability." More important than the actual scores are their implications for the child's functioning in different domains and need for help or special education.

Dynamic Assessment

Traditional use of tests is often referred to as "static" because the tests measure children's knowledge and skills at a particular point in time. From a social constructivist perspective on cognition, assessment should not only record which tasks the child does and does not master, but also the learning process. This implies identifying the child's zone of proximal development (see Book 4, *Cognition, Intelligence and Learning*, Part I) – what the child is able to do with help, and how much help is needed to solve a given task (Jeltova et al., 2007; Lidz, 1997). Guthke (1993) for example tested first-graders with a non-verbal cognitive test (Raven) in the traditional way; then the children received systematic and standardized help with tasks they were unable to solve on their own. Following this, they were tested once again with the Raven test, and the increase in their scores was interpreted as a measure of their *learning potential*. The study further showed that this increase correlated more closely with the children's math scores in later school grades than the ordinary test scores. Thus, dynamic testing measures not merely the child's skills at a given time but what the child learns under standard conditions.

Instruments for dynamic assessment include the **Learning Potential Assessment Device** (LPAD) (Feuerstein et al., 1997) and *Dynamic Assessment of Children's Narratives* (Miller et al., 2001). Dynamic assessments can be especially useful when children score low on tests and the results are inconsistent with other observations, when children come from a different culture and have problems with language, when children's performance seems to be low owing to learning disorders, emotional disorders and low motivation, and when the primary goal is not to categorize the child's ability level but to facilitate appropriate training. In this situation, it is important to know how the child understands and applies the principles associated with the tasks, and how much the child needs to learn in order to master different tasks (Tzuriel, 2005).

Response to Intervention

The evaluation of any measures that may have been initiated is an essential part of the assessment process. "Response to intervention" monitors whether the child's education yields the desired results and if there is a need for modifications or supplementing the ordinary education with other measures. The "response" can consist of academic improvement, but also better social and emotional functioning (Fox et al., 2010).

Both response to intervention and dynamic assessment include training and testing and thus share certain similarities. An important difference, however, is that dynamic assessment centers on the child's abilities using a *test–training–test* procedure, whereas response to intervention follows a *training–test–training* procedure. In a typical sequence of training and testing at different points in time, the two procedures are quite similar in practice, but the focus of dynamic assessment is on the child's abilities, whereas response to intervention focuses on the training (Lidz & Peña, 2009; Grigorenko, 2009).

Some researchers are critical of the widespread use of cognitive tests in schools. According to Floyd (2010), intelligence tests only serve as a general indication of whether a child has difficulties, a fact that is often known before the tests are taken. He believes that one gets more insight into children's problems by trying out different forms of intervention and observing the benefits of each, that is, the extent to which they reduce the child's difficulties. An assessment of this type can offer feedback to the child and help identify the learning strategies best suited to him or her (Clark, 2012). Positive feedback may also make the child more motivated to make extra effort in the domain(s) where he is struggling.

28

Ethical Considerations

Any observation of children involves a certain degree of intrusion into their privacy and sometimes into the family's life or the practice of professionals around the child. The most fundamental ethical issue is whether to conduct a study when weighing the potential benefits of gathering knowledge against the possible drawbacks and discomfort the study might entail. Because children are vulnerable and less able to assess the consequences of participating in a study than adults, a particular ethical responsibility rests with anyone conducting research on children. Parents must be given sufficient insight into the intent behind the research and the methods that will be used to be able to give their informed consent or refusal to the child's participation. Parents need to know that they can withdraw the child from the study at any time without the need for justification. Children must be given information they can understand and realize what they will be involved in, but children under 16 years of age should not give consent. Consent requires that they understand the consequences of saying yes or no to participation in the study, an understanding that children do not have (Koelch et al., 2009; Millum & Emanuel, 2007). Furthermore, it can be difficult for children to withdraw once they have given consent – they have promised an adult they will participate and are usually told that they should keep their promises. Children should know that their parents have given consent, so they can be sure that it is neither dangerous nor harmful for them to participate. Most countries have ethical research guidelines and ethical committees to assess whether a research project meets the necessary ethical criteria before the project can be launched.

DOI: 10.4324/9781003291275-31

Summary of Part III

1   Choice of method is determined by the information one wishes to obtain, the purpose of the study and its theoretical framework.
2   Observations are about what children and adults do. An observer can participate in activities or merely observe. Observations imply choosing one of several possible perspectives. Observations are divided into *categories* that are specified and defined. Categories must be unambiguous and are often mutually exclusive.
3   *Naturalistic observation* takes place in children's own environment and without influence by the observer. *Experiments* are carried out under *controlled* conditions. Laboratory experiments consist of customized situations. *Field experiments* combine naturalistic observation and experimental control. *Questionnaires* with close-ended questions or *archival studies* are often used to gather information about larger groups of children. *Interviews* can provide more detailed insight into children's and adults' thoughts and feelings.
4   *Quantitative methods* involve categorization, quantification, measurements and statistics and are suitable for research questions such as *who, what, when* and *how many*. *Qualitative methods* are used to describe processes and are suitable for research questions such as *why* and *how* something happens; processing typically involves text rather than numbers. *Microgenetic methods* combine quantitative and qualitative approaches. Mixed methods provide more information and a broader perspective.
5   *Group studies* compare children with different characteristics or children who are, or are not, exposed to a certain influence. The *experimental group* should correspond to the *control group* in every

way, except that the experimental group is exposed to the experimental treatment or influence.

6   *Case studies* describe individual children who have particular biological characteristics, grow up under particular conditions or receive a particular type of treatment. By going into greater depth, case studies represent a complement to group studies, but the findings can be difficult to generalize and apply to children in other contexts. Case studies are especially important to clinical developmental psychology.

7   *Cross-sectional studies* compare children at different age levels. *Longitudinal studies* observe the same group of children at two or more points in time. *Prospective studies* follow children over time. *Retrospective studies* are based on collecting past information, mostly from parents and others who know the children well. *Cross-cultural studies* compare children growing up in different cultures and offer a broad insight into the impact of the environment.

8   Studies of infants use *habituation* and *dishabituation*, *conditioning*, *visual exploration* (including *preferential looking*), as well as *physiological* and *neurophysiological measures*. The studies are important, but the results are often difficult to interpret, and there is significant disagreement about their implications for infants' cognitive skills and perception of their surroundings.

9   Research must be *transparent*, and all the details of the method must be openly available. The *sample* of children must be *representative* of the *population* they are part of. Methods must be *reliable* and *valid*, measure what they are intended to measure and provide answers to the questions raised. It is the validity that relates observations of children to understanding of their development.

10   An *assessment* is usually undertaken in response to a concern or referral. Methods include conversations and interviews, observations, tests and checklists. *Tests* are observations of children's ability to solve problems under predetermined conditions. Testing must be adapted to the individual child and requires test competency and good communication. *Dynamic assessment* focuses on the learning process and the child's learning potential. The results of an assessment are *interpreted*, *analyzed* and *collated*.

11   The most fundamental *ethical issue* behind all research is whether to conduct a study when weighing the potential benefits of gathering knowledge against any possible drawbacks and discomfort.

As children are vulnerable and unable to assess the consequences of participating in a study, a particular ethical responsibility rests with anyone conducting research on children. Parents must consent on behalf of their child, and children must be informed in a way they can understand. Ethical committees typically assess whether a research project meets the necessary ethical criteria before the project can be launched.

Core Issues

- The role of quantitative and qualitative methodology in scientific research.
- The lack of replicating studies.
- Consent, assent and the involvement of children in research.

Suggestions for Further Reading

Danby, S., Ewing, L., & Thorpe, K. (2011). The novice researcher: Interviewing young children. *Qualitative Inquiry*, *17*, 74–84.

Funamoto, A., & Rinaldi, C. M. (2015). Measuring parent–child mutuality: A review of current observational coding systems. *Infant Mental Health Journal*, *36*, 3–11.

Nosek, B. A., & Bar-Anan, Y. (2012). Scientific utopia: I. Opening scientific communication. *Psychological Inquiry*, *23*, 217–243.

Nosek, B. A., Spies, J. R., & Motyl, M. (2012). Scientific utopia: II. Restructuring incentives and practices to promote truth over publishability. *Perspectives on Psychological Science*, *7*, 615–631.

Robson, C., & McCartan, K. (2016). *Real world research, Fourth edition*. Chichester, UK: Wiley.

Sroufe, L. A., Egeland, B., Carlson, E., & Collins, W. A. (2005). *The development of the person: The Minnesota study of risk and adaptation from birth to adulthood*. New York, NY: Guilford Press.

Part IV

Child and Adolescent Disorders

Categorization of Disorders and Classification Systems

Categorization of Disorders

Part IV provides a brief description of the major diagnostic systems and the most common disorders in children and adolescents, and their prevalence. Issues related to the etiology and development of the disorders and their impact on development will be further discussed in the relevant chapters. The subject index at the end of the book is a useful tool for finding where a disorder is mentioned.

Knowledge about the basis for categorizing disorders is important for clinicians to be able to recognize, understand and communicate the problems children can experience (Rutter & Pine, 2015). Distinguishing characteristics are rarely absolute. Many disorders require the presence of only a certain number of the symptoms (Ortigo et al., 2010). Children who meet the criteria for a given disorder do not necessarily experience exactly the same problems or symptoms. In addition, there is a seamless transition between the normal variation in children's functioning and what constitutes a disorder.

Children with disorders are not characterized by their disorder(s) alone. In other areas they vary just as much as children without a disorder. Two children may meet the criteria for the same disorder and yet give very different impressions. Some children with autism spectrum disorders for example are passive and anxious, while others are active and seemingly without fear. Some lack speech, while others talk incessantly. In describing a child, it is important to detail the way in which the disorder manifests, as well as other traits and characteristics exhibited by the child, both those related to diagnosis and those specific to the individual.

DOI: 10.4324/9781003291275-33

Classification Systems

There are two main international classification systems for mental and behavioral disorders. The eleventh edition of *The International Statistical Classification of Diseases and Related Health Problems* (ICD-11) was published by the World Health Organization in 2018. (The ICD-11 browser is accessible at www.who.int/classifications/icd/en/.) The fifth edition of the *Diagnostic and Statistical Manual of Mental Disorders* (DSM-5) was published by the American Psychiatric Association in 2013. With each new edition, the two systems have become more similar, and ICD-11 resembles DSM-5 more than ICD-10. Many disorder categories have become more or less identical. Critical voices however believe that ICD-11 should avoid the weaknesses of DSM-5 (Roessner et al., 2016) – among other things the fact that the threshold for a number of diagnoses has either been lowered or raised, and that many of the categories in DSM-5 have not been sufficiently tested (Frances & Nardo, 2013). The differences between ICD and DSM and the changes in the diagnostic systems over time emphasize that diagnoses are not "natural" entities but conventional categories that can be changed with new theoretical and empirical insights.

DC 0–3: Diagnostic Classification of Mental Health and Developmental Disorders of Infancy and Early Childhood (Zero to Three; Wieder, 1994) is a supplement to ICD and DSM for the diagnosis of children below the age of 3 years.

The International Classification of Functioning, Disability and Health (ICF) (World Health Organization, 2001) describes children's and adults' health by using a more comprehensive approach, independent of diagnosis. This includes both physical and mental functions and distinguishes between *functioning and disability* on the one hand and *environmental factors* on the other. As *activity* and *participation* are directly associated with functioning and disability, an individual's activities and participation are key elements in the characterization of disabilities. *Disability* is defined as a deviation from what is possible or common, related to impaired body function, restricted activity or limited participation.

ICF is published in a separate version for children and young people: *International Classification of Functioning, Disability and Health, Children and Youth Version* (ICF-CY) (World Health Organization, 2007). It includes a number of topics specifically related to childhood, such as *temperament and personality functions, acquiring language,* and *learning through actions with objects.* The child's age is taken into account in the coding of functions and deviations (Björck-Åkesson et al., 2010).

It may be useful to combine ICF and ICF-CY with ICD and DSM (Selb et al., 2015).

30

Sensory Impairments

Sensory impairment primarily involves vision and hearing, also in combination with each other. Milder impairments of vision and hearing can be difficult to detect, especially as children have no way of knowing how other children see and hear. Mostly, they have never experienced normal vision or hearing before. Early diagnosis is important for the creation of an environment that provides the children with access to experiences that allow them to establish social relations and create meaning based on their own perceptual abilities.

Visual Impairment

Mild visual impairments are common, and most of them can easily be corrected with glasses. Approximately 1–2 percent of schoolchildren have reduced vision with functional consequences. In Western countries, congenital blindness and severe visual impairment have a prevalence rate of about 1 in 2,000. In countries with less favorable economic conditions, the prevalence rate is higher, about 15 in 10,000 (Dale & Edwards, 2015). Some children have *perceptual problems* caused by injury or disturbances in the eye's motor function or the development of the brain. Children with *cortical visual impairment* can see and follow objects, but have difficulty processing visual information and recognizing people and objects (Fazzi et al., 2012).

Many children with severe visual impairment have additional disorders, particularly mobility and hearing impairment, and intellectual disability (Geddie et al., 2013). Although rare, *juvenile neuronal ceroid lipofuscinosis* (JNCL, or **Batten disease**) continues to be the most common cause of blindness in many countries in children aged 5–15

DOI: 10.4324/9781003291275-34

years. Development is normal during the first few years, but a gradual loss of vision sets in at the age of 4–5 years, eventually followed by the loss of cognitive, language and motor functions. JNCL is associated with early death, usually in late adolescence or early adulthood (Mole et al., 2011).

Hearing Impairment

Hearing impairment is commonly rated by the degree of hearing loss: deafness (above 95 dB), profound hearing loss (70–95 dB), severe hearing loss (60–70 dB), moderate hearing loss (40–60 dB) and mild hearing loss (10–40 dB). However, children's hearing shows major variations, and the decibel scale does not always provide a good indication of a child's hearing functions. *Hard of hearing* means that the child can comprehend and develop speech with a hearing aid, and *deafness* that the hearing loss is too great for speech to be perceived even with a hearing aid.

An important distinction is that between *prelingual* and *acquired hearing loss*. Hearing loss after children have developed spoken language has other developmental consequences than hearing loss that is congenital or occurs before speech has evolved. Another distinction is that between conductive and neurogenic hearing loss. *Conductive hearing loss* is usually caused by defects or injury to the middle ear, or by fluid obstructing the transfer of movement from the eardrum to the inner ear. It is easy to treat, but even minor but prolonged hearing loss can affect a child's vocabulary and knowledge acquisition. During preschool age, 12–14 percent of all children experience some form of reduced hearing for shorter or longer periods, mostly caused by ear infections and fluid in the inner ear. *Neurogenic hearing loss* refers to damage or defects in the inner ear, the auditory nerve or the brain. About two in every 1,000 children have a moderate hearing loss, and one in 1,000 is born deaf (Dietz et al., 2009).

Half of all incidents of profound early neurogenic hearing loss are probably related to genetic factors, but only 5–10 percent of deaf children have deaf parents. Infections and childhood diseases can lead to deafness (Dietz et al., 2009). About 40 percent of children with profound hearing impairment have other disorders such as ADHD, autism spectrum disorders, intellectual disabilities and learning disorders (Mitchell & Karchmer, 2006).

Deafblindness

A combination of early profound vision and hearing loss is quite rare, with a prevalence of 1 in 29,000 (Dammeyer, 2010). The cause is often unknown and may be related to genetic factors, prenatal infections, substance abuse by the mother or a number of different **syndromes** (Dammeyer, 2014; Wright, 2008). About 5 percent of all children with profound hearing loss have Usher syndrome, which leads to the eye disorder retinitis pigmentosa as well as problems with balance (Bitner-Glindzicz & Saihan, 2013).

31

Motor Impairments

Children may have reduced gross or fine motor control, or both (see Book 2, *Genes, Fetal Development and Early Neurological Development*, Part III). The most common causes of motor impairment in children and adolescents are **cerebral palsy**, spina bifida and injury from accidents. A number of illnesses and syndromes affect motor control, such as spinal muscular atrophy (Moultrie et al., 2016; Tisdale & Pellizzoni, 2015) and Duchenne muscular dystrophy (Emery et al., 2015; Flanigan, 2012). Additionally, neurological coordination disorders and **dyspraxia** can affect the performance of motor actions but do not involve paralysis or motor impairment in the conventional sense (Gibbs et al., 2007a).

Cerebral Palsy

Cerebral palsy (CP) is caused by a congenital or early acquired injury to the brain that results in various degrees of motor impairment (Rosenbaum et al., 2007). In the industrialized world, about 2 in every 1,000 children have cerebral palsy, with widely varying degrees of severity (Blair, 2010). Some children's impairments are so mild as to be nearly invisible in daily life, while others must rely on a wheelchair. Spastic CP accounts for about 80 percent of all cases and is characterized by a general increase in muscular tension. It is graded according to the extent of motor impairment (Hoon & Tolley, 2012). Children with cerebral palsy have a higher prevalence of cognitive and language disorders than the general population, but there is considerable variation within this group (Stadskleiv et al., 2017).

DOI: 10.4324/9781003291275-35

Spina Bifida

Spina bifida, also called *cleft spine*, is a congenital sac-like bulge of nerve tissue due to an incomplete closing of the vertebrae during fetal development. Its prevalence is about 1 in 10,000 births. The impairment of primary motor functions is related to the location and size of the sac. The amount of cerebrospinal fluid around the brain and spinal cord is affected, and many children need a surgical insertion of a *shunt*, a valve that regulates the pressure caused by the accumulation of fluid in the brain (Mitchell et al., 2004). Some children with spina bifida have problems with orientation, attention regulation, coordination of movements and speech (Dennis et al., 2006; Huber-Okrainec et al., 2005).

Developmental Coordination Disorder

Developmental coordination disorder in DSM-5, developmental motor coordination disorder in ICD-11, or *dyspraxia* presents early in life, and children experience varying degrees of difficulty planning, organizing, executing and automating actions under voluntary control, especially when someone is watching them. Unintelligible speech is common. The prevalence rate is somewhat uncertain, estimated at 5–6 percent during infancy and 2 percent for more severe conditions. It is two to seven times more common in boys than in girls (Gibbs et al., 2007a; Macintyre, 2000, 2001). Both ICD-11 and DSM-5 categorize this disorder under the broader heading of neurodevelopmental disorders, and it occurs frequently together with other disorders in this group (Steinman et al., 2010).

32

Neurodevelopmental Disorders

Neurodevelopmental disorders begin in early childhood and have a varied course of progression clearly related to the organism's maturation and development *as well as* to the influence of experience (Thapar & Rutter, 2015). They include intellectual disability, communication and language disorders, autism spectrum disorders, attention deficit disorders, reading and writing disorders, mathematics disorders, a number of motor disorders, tic disorders, schizophrenia and other psychoses, with some variation between ICD-11 and DSM-5.

An important reason for defining neurodevelopmental disorders as a higher-order category is the considerable coincidence in symptoms. Co-occurrence of two or more disorders is commonly referred to as *comorbidity*, based on the assumption that they are independent conditions. However, neurodevelopmental disorders occur far more frequently together than one would expect based on sheer coincidence, and there is reason to believe that they share some common basis or processes that affect each other during development. While different disorders can share underlying weaknesses or vulnerabilities, different developmental paths can also lead to the same disorder (Thapar & Rutter, 2015).

Language Disorders

Approximately 6–12 percent of all children have delayed language development or language impairment, and 1–2 percent have severe language disorders. Some children have problems with speech, others with the language itself. The disorders are two to three times more common among boys than girls (Cummings, 2008; Weindrich et al., 2000).

DOI: 10.4324/9781003291275-36

Several systems for categorizing language disorders are in use. ICD-11 includes *developmental speech sound disorder, developmental speech fluency disorder* and *language disorders* with impairment of (a) **receptive** and **expressive language**, (b) mainly expressive language, (c) mainly pragmatic language and (d) other specified or unspecified language impairments. DSM-5 distinguishes between *language disorders, speech sound disorders, childhood-onset fluency disorders, social (pragmatic) communication disorders* and *unspecified communication disorders*. The categories listed in ICD-11 and DSM-5 are too general to be of use in practical work however. Practitioners who work specifically with language disorders subdivide them in far greater detail (Cummings, 2008). Children with *phonological disorders* have difficulty perceiving and producing speech sounds, while children with *articulation disorders* have problems with the physical production of sound itself. *Grammatical impairments* involve problems with sentence formation and conjugation. *Semantic impairments* entail problems with the contents of language, and *pragmatic disorders* with the communication and use of language itself, such as understanding others' intentions, the choice of topic, repairing gaps in communication and maintaining a coherent conversation. Even children with good pronunciation or correct sentence structure may have an inadequate understanding of how language can be used (Cummings, 2014). Additionally, there are *voice difficulties* and *fluency disorders* such as *stuttering* and *cluttering* (Cummings, 2008; Simms, 2007). Language disorders are not necessarily linked to speech – some children with hearing impairments show similar difficulties when using sign language (Morgan et al., 2007).

Many factors can affect typical and atypical language development. When no clear evidence of a language disorder can be found and development proceeds normally in other areas, language impairments are considered to be "specific." Per definition, children with a specific language impairment do not have hearing loss, autism spectrum disorder, intellectual disability, brain damage, physical disabilities or other difficulties that could explain their language problems. Specific language impairment (SLI) is thus defined by exclusion (Bishop, 2006). Because language development is influenced by a large number of factors, language and communication problems can be found in children with various disorders such as ADHD, hearing impairment, motor impairment, intellectual disability and autism spectrum disorders (Conti-Ramsden et al., 2006; Turner & Stone, 2007).

Learning Disorders

Learning disorders are related to the educational objectives of society. They include impairments in reading, written expression, mathematics and other specified impairments of learning, or unspecified developmental learning disorders. Intellectual disability is not included in this category (see below). DSM-5 refers to them as "specific," meaning there is a gap between the expectations of the child's learning based on general cognitive functioning (usually based on IQ test scores) and the child's actual performance in a specific area of skill or knowledge. For example, a child can score well above average on an intelligence test and at the same time have major difficulties learning to read, write or do arithmetic (Ruban & Reis, 2005). It can be problematic however to distinguish between specific and general disorders, such as between a mild intellectual disability and an emotional disorder, or between a learning disorder and underachievement (Algozzine et al., 2012; Kavale et al., 2005).

Reading and Writing Disorders

Many children struggle to learn how to read and write, but most of them manage to do so within the usual period of time (Åsberg et al., 2010). Inadequate training does not provide grounds for diagnosing a reading or writing disorder, such as in the case of children growing up in war without a functioning educational system. Prevalence is generally estimated at 7 percent, although this depends on the definition used (Peterson & Pennington, 2015). The prevalence rate diminishes with age, but a third of all children diagnosed with dyslexia at the age of 8 still meet the criteria years later. Some children have reading comprehension problems throughout school age (Woolley, 2010). There are many weak readers, but it is not known how many children fail to acquire basic reading skills altogether. Just like language disorders, reading and writing disorders are more common among boys than girls, and a number of boys develop persistent problems (Shaywitz et al., 2008; Wheldall & Limbrick, 2010).

Studies have found a clear connection between early language disorders and reading and writing disorders, although not all children with developmental language disorders experience persistent problems reading and writing (Ricketts, 2011). It appears that the types of problems associated with children's language acquisition also represent obstacles in learning how to read and write. Children with *phonological* problems may find it difficult to learn to read words and spell. Children with problems understanding the content of language also show similar problems in regard to reading (Bishop & Snowling, 2004). The importance of phonological problems can vary between languages, and it is by no means certain whether all results from the predominantly English-language research can be generalized to more phonetically written languages. Reading places relatively small demands on visual perception. The alphabet consists of a limited number of characters, and there is no evidence that visual processing represents an obstacle to learning how to read or that visual training will help children with reading disorders (Handler et al., 2011).

Some children can read aloud but do not understand what they are reading. The precocious ability to read far above one's own comprehension level is known as **hyperlexia**. This group includes children with specific reading disorders, autism spectrum disorders, language disorders and intellectual disability (Grigorenko et al., 2003; Nation & Norbury, 2005).

Mathematics Disorders

Mathematics disorders, or *dyscalculia*, involve major difficulties understanding numbers and mathematical concepts and solving arithmetic problems. Children can experience difficulties with simple tasks such as counting small dots or using their fingers in basic addition or subtraction tasks at an age when other children remember the answer or quickly do a mental calculation. Between 3 and 6 percent of all children are estimated to have a mathematics disorder, depending on the criteria used (Butterworth, 2008; Gifford & Rockliffe, 2012). A larger proportion of children and adolescents struggle with math and receive regular help without being considered to have a particular disorder. Special difficulties with mathematics can be found in many groups, among others in children with a low birth weight, ADHD, dyspraxia, dyslexia, cerebral palsy and epilepsy, and those who have problems with memory, perception and sequencing (Gifford & Rockliffe, 2012; Green & Gallagher, 2014). A relationship has been found between the degree of mathematical disorders on the one hand and spatial perception, sense of direction, working memory and other executive functions on the other (Miller et al., 2013; Raghubar et al., 2010; Tosto et al., 2014).

Intellectual Disability

The terminology used in connection with more extensive general disorders of development and learning is undergoing constant change. DSM-5 uses the term "intellectual disability," and ICD-11 "disorders of intellectual development."

ICD-11 includes four levels of intellectual disability, based on IQ and **adaptive function**. In mild intellectual disability, adaptive function and IQ are 2–3 **standard deviations** below the mean (IQ 69–55) (see Book 4, *Cognition, Intelligence and Learning*, Chapter 26) and, in moderate intellectual disability, 3–4 standard deviations below the mean (IQ 54–40). In both severe and profound disability, intellectual functioning is more than 4 standard deviations below the mean (IQ 39 and lower). Severe and profound disorders of intellectual development are differentiated exclusively on the basis of **adaptive behavior** differences because existing standardized tests of intelligence cannot reliably or validly distinguish among individuals with intellectual functioning below 4 standard deviations. DSM-5 considers IQ to be an approximate expression for the ability to form concepts and to reason and does not use IQ in the classification of intellectual disabilities. Instead, it describes conceptual, social and practical skills according to the same four levels of intellectual and adaptive functioning used by ICD-11: mild, moderate, severe and profound. Intelligence tests continue to be important tools for assessing problems, but, in DSM-5, children who achieve a full-scale IQ of over 70 can also meet the criteria for intellectual disability. Caution is indicated, especially for younger children, whose test scores tend to be less stable. In addition, one cannot use a full-scale IQ as a basis for the diagnosis when the profile is skewed, as this mean score may provide a false indication of both what the child masters and what the child is unable to do (Greenspan & Woods, 2014). For example, one 13-year-old girl scored average for her age on non-verbal subscales and did not master any items on the verbal subscales. An IQ in the middle would give a too low estimate of her non-verbal skills and a too high estimate of her verbal skills.

Based on a statistical definition, intelligence has a **normal distribution** curve. This means that about 2 percent of a population have an intellectual disability, meaning an IQ below 70 (see Book 4, *Cognition, Intelligence and Learning*, Chapter 26). Within this group, the distribution is about 85 percent mild, 10 percent moderate, 3–4 percent severe and 1–2 percent profound. However, prevalence studies of intellectual disability show a significantly lower percentage (less than 1 per cent), and mild intellectual disability usually lies below 50 percent (Carr & O'Reilly, 2016a; Strømme & Valvatne, 1998). This is partly owing to the fact that many children with a mild intellectual disability are able to manage on their own, possibly with the help of the family, and have therefore never been assessed or diagnosed.

Autism Spectrum Disorders

Autism spectrum disorder is a pervasive developmental disorder characterized by problems related to communication and social interaction, as well as restricted, repetitive and stereotyped interests and behaviors. The disorder emerges in childhood, but the former requirement that symptoms should be present before the age of 3 has been abandoned in ICD-11 and DSM-5, as many of the problems of children with autism spectrum disorders and a high degree of **language function** may not become apparent and may remain undiagnosed until early school age. Earlier subcategories such as *infantile autism*, *Asperger syndrome* and *atypical autism* are no longer part of the diagnostic group. In both ICD-11 and DSM-5, *autism spectrum disorder* has become a collective term with possibilities of specifying if the individual has intellectual disability and language impairment or is lacking speech. Autism spectrum disorder is a heterogeneous condition with a genetic basis and significant variation in developmental trajectories (Lord et al., 2015).

Prevalence figures for autism spectrum disorder have increased significantly since childhood autism was first described by Kanner (1943), from 1 in 10,000 to 15 in 1,000 in 2015. The reason for this increase has been the subject of much discussion, and most experts agree that it partly reflects the expansion of diagnostic criteria, increasing attention on high-functioning children within this group, earlier diagnosis and the awareness that autism spectrum disorder is a lifelong condition (Matson & Kozlowski, 2011). At least twice as many boys as girls have autism spectrum disorder.

Children with autism spectrum disorder show considerable variation in intelligence and symptoms (Hughes, 2009; Volkmar et al., 2014). Approximately two-thirds score within or above the normal range (above IQ 70) on intelligence tests. Language skills can vary from little communicative ability to the use of more or less well-formed sentences (Rapin et al., 2009). The diagnostic criteria entail that all children with the diagnosis have greater problems than other children understanding emotions and reasoning about how other people think and feel and why they act as they do, including those with highly developed verbal abilities (Hoogenhout & Malcolm-Smith, 2014).

Attention Deficit Disorders

ICD-11 and DSM-5 categorize **attention deficit hyperactivity disorder (ADHD)** in the same manner. It consists of three elements that manifest in different ways throughout childhood and into adulthood: attention deficit, **hyperactivity** and impulsivity – they don't think before they act. Usually, children with this diagnosis are characterized not by a general lack of attention but by the inability to *sustain attention*. This, however, can vary significantly with activity and interests (Rothenberger & Banaschewski, 2007). Girls are less active and more inattentive than boys, and their attention deficits are frequently overlooked as they have a different expression than in restless boys (Cardoos & Hinshaw, 2011; Skogli et al., 2013).

One subtype presents predominantly with hyperactivity and impulsivity. Children with this subtype display a particularly high level of activity and impulsivity and little sustained attention. They are restless and may experience problems with emotional regulation, motor coordination, working memory, spatial perception and executive function and have a somewhat delayed language development. They typically score in the lower part of the normal range on intelligence tests (Shaw et al., 2014).

The second subtype presents predominantly with inattention. The children do not show the same degree of restlessness, but are poorly organized and have little perseverance, in addition to difficulties with working memory and motor coordination. Some hyperactive-impulsive symptoms may be present, but these are less significant compared with the symptoms of inattention (Sonuga-Barke & Taylor, 2015).

Children with the third subtype present with a combination: inattention, hyperactivity and impulsivity are all clinically significant.

There is a significant overlap between attention deficit disorder and other neurodevelopmental disorders (Biederman, 2005). Children with attention deficit disorders often show stronger emotional reactions than other children and are susceptible to developing **oppositional defiant disorder** (Frick & Nigg, 2012; Lambek et al., 2017).

The prevalence of attention deficit disorder varies considerably and in many countries has increased during the 2000s (Hinshaw, 2018). A prevalence rate of over 5 percent has been reported for preschool age children (Nomura et al., 2014). Common estimates are 2–5 percent between the ages of 6 and 16 years and somewhat lower for adults. Approximately three times as many boys get an ADHD diagnosis compared with girls, resulting in a prevalence rate of about 9 percent for boys and under 3 percent for girls (Rothenberger & Banaschewski, 2004). There is no clear boundary between actions that are part of the common variation in activity level and actions that indicate a disorder in need of intervention. Some experts express concern that too many children receive this diagnosis (Cormier, 2008; Frick & Nigg, 2012).

Behavioral and Emotional Disorders

Behavioral disorders and emotional disorders are broad diagnostic terms, and it is important to distinguish normal and slightly unregulated behavior from what may be defined as a disorder, such as common testing of limits or adolescent rebelliousness versus oppositional defiant disorders. **Externalizing disorders** include destructive, bullying, fraudulent and aggressive actions of such scope that they become disruptive to children and adults in the environment and require intervention. **Internalizing disorders** include mood and anxiety disorders.

Behavioral Disorders

Behavioral disorders can assume many forms and varying degrees of severity. In ICD-11, *disruptive behavior and dissocial disorders* are characterized by persistent behaviors that range from defiant, disobedient, provocative or spiteful behaviors to actions that violate the basic rights of others or major age-appropriate societal norms, rules or laws. The behavior pattern is of sufficient severity to result in significant impairment in personal, family, social, educational, occupational or other important areas of functioning. Onset is usually but not always in childhood. In mild form, the child exhibits few negative actions beyond what is needed to establish a diagnosis, and actions are of little harm to others. In moderate form, the number of actions increases, and their negative impact on others becomes clearer. The severe form includes numerous negative actions that can cause considerable harm to others. In a minority of cases, behavioral disorders are accompanied by an insufficiently developed sense of **conscience** and guilt and, at times, also a lack of empathy or indifference in relation to the damage caused by the behavior (Williams & Hill, 2012).

DOI: 10.4324/9781003291275-37

There are two subtypes: oppositional defiant disorder and conduct-dissocial disorder. *Oppositional defiant disorder* presents markedly defiant, disobedient, provocative or spiteful behavior that occurs more frequently than is typically observed in individuals at the same developmental level and that is not restricted to interaction with siblings. It is a persistent pattern that has lasted 6 months or more. The disorder may be manifest in prevailing, persistent angry or irritable mood, often accompanied by severe temper outbursts, or in headstrong, argumentative and defiant behavior. *Conduct-dissocial disorder* is characterized by a repetitive and persistent pattern of behavior in which the basic rights of others or major age-appropriate societal norms, rules or laws are violated. This includes aggression toward people or animals, destruction of property, deceitfulness or theft, and serious violations of rules. To be diagnosed, the behavior pattern must endure for 12 months or more. Isolated dissocial or criminal acts are thus not in themselves grounds for the diagnosis.

In DSM-5, the main category of *disruptive, impulse-control and conduct disorders* includes several disorders that need not be mutually exclusive. Children with *oppositional defiant disorder* have problems regulating their emotions, are irritable, easily throw tantrums and can be malicious and vindictive when they meet resistance. They are reluctant to do what authorities tell them to and to follow normal rules. Conflicts with adults are common. Problems often begin to show up during preschool age, but can also appear as late as adolescence. Some children show behavioral problems in certain situations only, and the degree of severity depends on the number of situations in which the child shows negative behavior.

Intermittent explosive disorder is a type of **emotion regulation** *disorder* characterized by anger and poor impulse control, particularly in the form of language and physical actions that can harm others. The diagnosis requires the child to be above the age of 6 years and to function cognitively above this age level, as younger children usually are not able to self-regulate well enough. The disorder mostly occurs in later childhood, adolescence and adulthood. In certain situations, it may be natural for the child to react, but the reaction is completely out of proportion in relation to the event that triggered it.

The features of *conduct disorder* in DSM-5 are similar to those of *conduct-dissocial disorder* in ICD-11. They may include bullying; initiation of physical fights; use of a knife, a gun or other weapon that can cause serious physical harm; physical cruelty to people or animals;

destruction; deceitfulness; theft; truanting from school; and serious violations of rules.

There is considerable overlap between the characteristics of various behavioral disorders. It is possible that behavioral disorders represent a dimension that varies with the type and extent of negative actions, rather than distinct categories (Scott, 2015). Prevalence estimates vary, but mostly lie between 5 and 10 percent. The prevalence is two to three times higher among boys than girls (Odgers et al., 2008).

Mood Disorders

Mood disorders, or *affective disorders*, are the most frequent psychological disorders among children and adolescents. They mainly include depression, mania and bipolar disorder. Mood disorders can occur at any age and are also included in DC 0–3.

Depression

Most children and adolescents can feel sad or unhappy at times. To meet the criteria for depression, changes in mood must last for weeks or months. In toddlers, depression shows up in the form of despondency or **irritability** and reduced interest and pleasure in activities suited to the child's developmental level. The child may have decreased appetite and difficulty sleeping (Witten, 1997). Similarly, children and adolescents show less pleasure, interest and concentration than they normally would and easily become tired. They sleep poorly and have little appetite, low **self-esteem** and little confidence. Depressed adolescents tend to ruminate and have problems coping with their emotions and taking pleasure in activities they usually enjoy. Depression can become deeper when it leads to social isolation and fewer friends. The inability of adolescents to solve the problems they meet may contribute to stress, a poor self-image and dysphoria (Hankin et al., 2018). Depression in children and adolescents must have lasted for a year to be considered *persistent*. Following the loss of a parent or other caregiver, toddlers can show a *prolonged grief reaction* lasting for more than 2 weeks (Lieberman et al., 2003; Tidmarsh, 1997). In *persistent depressive disorder* or *dysthymic disorder*, the depressive mood is persistent, lasting continuously 2 years or more and for most of the day or for more days than not. In children and adolescents the depressed mood can manifest as pervasive irritability.

Depression can also express itself in agitated and disruptive behavior. According to DSM-5, *disruptive mood dysregulation disorder* is characterized by "severe recurrent temper outbursts manifested verbally and/or behaviorally," often as a reaction to frustration, but in a way that is inconsistent with the child's age. Because younger children generally have problems with self-regulation, children under the age of 6 years cannot receive this diagnosis, nor can young adults above the age of 18. The criteria require outbursts at least three to four times a week, in connection with a minimum of three different situations and having taken place for over a year. According to DSM-5, the prevalence rate is 2–5 percent and primarily involves boys.

Depression is relatively rare during childhood but increases toward adolescence. In preschool age, the prevalence is estimated at 1 percent, and at 3 percent in school age. With a prevalence rate of 10 percent during adolescence, depression is the most common reason for young people to seek help for their personal problems. Up to a quarter of all adolescents report having experienced at least one depressive episode (Garber & Rao, 2014). However, it is important to distinguish between depression that meets the diagnostic criteria and the uncertainty and dysphoria that often characterize young people without justifying the term depression. In childhood, depression occurs just as frequently in boys as in girls, but, during adolescence, its prevalence is twice as high in girls (Hankin & Abramson, 2001).

Bipolar Disorder

Bipolar disorder is characterized by depressive periods and periods of mania. Manic periods can include agitation, little need for sleep, impulsivity, risky behavior and uncritical thinking. Bipolar disorder usually first appears in early adulthood, but can also occur in children, in which case it is referred to as *paediatric bipolar disorder* (Fitzgerald & Pavuluri, 2015). However, there is considerable discussion about the existence of bipolar disorder in children, and DSM-5 emphasizes the difficulty of diagnosing the disorder during childhood. It is especially difficult to establish clear periods of euphoria and mania. Distinct episodes of depression and mania usually do not occur in childhood, but rather a mixture of depression, agitation and irritability (Carr, 2016). Symptoms related to ADHD in particular can be misinterpreted as bipolar disorder, as the two diagnoses share many traits, including distractibility, talkativeness and a high activity level (Leibenluft &

Dickstein, 2015). Also, in adolescents, bipolar disorder can be difficult to detect because it can develop gradually without any apparent periods of illness. Children and adolescents with this disorder frequently show problems across the entire social spectrum, and it may additionally share common traits with autism spectrum disorder (Fitzgerald & Pavuluri, 2015). The prevalence rate is about 1 percent and equally divided among boys and girls (Carr, 2016).

Anxiety or Fear-Related Disorders

Anxiety disorders mainly consist of separation anxiety, phobias (including social phobia or anxiety) and generalized anxiety disorder. Anxiety disorders occur at all ages and are also listed in DC 0–3. The diagnosis is difficult to establish in younger children however, because anxiety and fear are common at this age and may represent an adequate adaptation to an uncertain and potentially threatening situation, or one perceived as such by the child. It is the intensity of anxiety or fear and its persistence once the uncertain situation has passed that characterize abnormal fear (Pine & Klein, 2015). Toddlers may react by crying, screaming and throwing themselves on the floor, as well as by angry outbursts that lead them to throw their toys and bump their head in connection with transitions, separations and changes in routines. The prevalence of anxiety disorders in children and adolescents is estimated at somewhere between 6 and 10 percent and slightly higher among boys than girls (Carr, 2016; Pine & Klein, 2015). Anxiety symptoms are common in children and adolescents with autism spectrum disorder (Kerns & Kendall, 2014).

Separation Anxiety

Central to separation anxiety is the fear of being separated from attachment figures (see Book 7, *Social Relations, Self-awareness and Identity*, Chapter 4). In toddlers, the reactions to such a separation, or the worry that a separation will occur in the future, must be stronger and more persistent than normal. Children may cling to caregivers and react with angry outbursts, kicking, screaming and crying when someone tries to separate them. They may be reluctant or refuse to sleep away from the attachment figure and have recurrent nightmares about separation. Children may also experience physical symptoms when leaving for kindergarten or school, or in other ways refuse to go to school. Adolescents can be anxious to be left at home alone. Symptoms usually appear in childhood, and DSM-5 specifies 18 years as the upper age limit. Symptoms must last longer than 4 weeks in children and adolescents, and 6 months in adults. The prevalence rate is about 3 percent (Carr, 2016). Separation anxiety is the most common anxiety disorder in children below the age of 12 years, and symptoms can continue all the way into adult age, such as a reluctance to sleep away from home or go out alone, but separation anxiety is rare in adults (Pine & Klein, 2015).

Phobias

Childhood phobias are characterized by recurring fears that are more persistent and intense than normal fear in children. A diagnosis requires the fear to have consequences for the child's ability to function socially. The onset of phobias can occur at any age, but usually they first appear during childhood. Common phobias among children may involve things such as syringes, animals or blood, or specific locations such as elevators. Children can react with clinging behavior and crying, but also with anger and active avoidance, feeling that they do not get help regulating their response. The prevalence rate for simple phobias is 3 percent, and 1 percent for social phobia (Carr, 2016).

Social Anxiety Disorder

This disorder is characterized by a stronger fear of strangers than normal for a given age and by apprehension or anxiety in unfamiliar social situations. The intensity of anxiety must be of such a degree as to create problems in social interaction with other children and adults. Occasional instances of anxiety are not enough. Children with social anxiety nearly always show great distress when they meet strangers and may not be able to do anything when many people are present. In such situations, they tend to cry, cling to familiar adults, withdraw and turn silent. Older children and adolescents are afraid that others will perceive them negatively, such as being incompetent, stupid, weak and dull. Children with social anxiety generally try to avoid social situations. According to DSM-5, the prevalence rate lies well above 2 percent and decreases with age. The first symptoms of social anxiety usually appear between the ages of 8 and

15 years, and early development is often characterized by shyness (Kagan & Snidman, 2004).

Generalized Anxiety Disorder

Generalized anxiety disorder (GAD) is most common among adults but can occur in children and adolescents. It is characterized by persistent anxiety and worry lasting for at least 6 months in connection with several situations that are difficult to cope with. Children may for example be unreasonably worried about disasters, not being liked, not managing their schoolwork or being teased. These concerns can be accompanied by fatigue, restlessness, irritability and sleep problems (Weems & Varela, 2011). The results may be little play and interaction with other children, and stress and worries that draw on cognitive resources and divert attention from other activities.

Selective Mutism

Children with selective (or elective) mutism only speak at home and with their immediate family. Symptoms usually appear before the age of 5, with a prevalence rate below 1 percent (Carr, 2016; Bergman et al., 2002). Some children with selective mutism experience early difficulties with language, but the diagnosis requires the child to be able to talk. Lack of motivation is not an underlying factor. Children with selective mutism want to speak but are unable to do so. Many of them are generally shy and socially anxious and therefore incapable of speaking with others, including friends, grandparents or more distant relatives. ICD-11 and DSM-5 require symptoms to persist for at least 1 month. As many children do not speak for a long period after beginning at school, the diagnosis is usually given only once the child has failed to speak for far longer than a month (Cline & Baldwin, 2004; Steinhausen et al., 2006). The problem is specifically associated with speech, and it is possible in some cases to communicate via writing or graphic symbols.

Obsessive-Compulsive Disorder

The main characteristics of obsessive-compulsive disorder (OCD) consist of recurrent thoughts and impulses to perform specific actions, such as repeated hand washing or licking a dish. The disorder is usually accompanied by anxiety, and the individual's compulsive actions are intended to avert a situation that is perceived to be dangerous. Because they can be observed, compulsive actions are easier to identify than obsessive thoughts, which must be determined based on conversation. The average age for onset of initial symptoms is 19 years, but in a quarter of all cases symptoms appear before the age of 14 years. As a rule, the disorder is more serious when it shows up early (Anholt et al., 2014). Compulsive behavior is often permanent but can be more or less pronounced in periods. According to DSM-5, the prevalence rate is 1–2 percent. OCD is commonly associated with **inhibition** and internalizing disorders and often comorbid with other conditions, including various anxiety disorders, attention deficit disorder, autism spectrum disorder and Tourette syndrome (Brem et al., 2014).

Eating Disorders

Eating disorders have many similarities with OCD, but the obsessive thoughts revolve exclusively around food, body, appearance and weight. The most common among these disorders are **anorexia**, involving under-eating, and **bulimia**, involving binge-eating and "countermeasures" against food intake such as intentional regurgitation or use of a laxative. Eating disorders are often accompanied by fear of obesity (Clinton, 2010) and negative thoughts about oneself (Yiend et al., 2014). The prevalence rate is 3 in 1,000 for anorexia, 9 in 1,000 for bulimia and 16 in 1,000 for binge-eating. The disorder typically appears around 14–18 years of age but can occur as early as the age of 6. The prevalence rate during childhood however is merely 3 in 100,000. Problems tend to be more extensive and persistent when they appear early. Eating disorders occur in boys, but are six times more frequent in girls (Pinhas et al., 2011).

34

Trauma and Stressor-Related Disorders

These types of disorders are the result of traumatic experiences or childhood environments with extremely poor caregiving.

Reactive Attachment Disorder

This disorder is characterized by grossly abnormal attachment behaviors in early childhood. The children are inhibited and emotionally withdrawn from their caregivers. They rarely seek comfort when distressed and show minimal response to comfort. They exhibit persistent social and emotional disturbance, with little social and emotional responsiveness, minimal positive affect and episodes of unexplained fearfulness and irritability, even when interacting with adults in situations without apparent threat. Diagnosis requires that the child has experienced patterns of serious neglect and repeated changes of caregivers or limited opportunities to form selective attachment relationships. The disorder emerges between the ages of 9 months and 5 years (but should not be diagnosed before the age of 1) and may persist for several years. Its prevalence is unknown.

Disinhibited Social Engagement Disorder

Children with this disorder actively seek interaction with unfamiliar adults. They show little reticence and can go off with a stranger without hesitation. They overstep the social boundaries of their culture, both physically by seeking excessive closeness and verbally by asking personal and intrusive questions. They do not check back with their caregiver when venturing into unfamiliar surroundings. Diagnosis requires that the child has experienced patterns of serious neglect

DOI: 10.4324/9781003291275-38

and repeated changes of caregivers or limited opportunities to form selective attachment relationships. Additionally, the child must have a **mental age** of at least 9 months and thus the cognitive prerequisites to form attachments. The disorder occurs only in connection with neglect before the age of 2 years; it emerges in the second year of life and lasts until adolescence (Guyon-Harris et al., 2018). Its prevalence is unknown.

Post-Traumatic Stress Disorder

Post-traumatic stress disorder (PTSD) is a reaction to a stressful or traumatic event a child has experienced or learned about. The diagnosis requires the occurrence of a real event, such as divorce, death in the family or witnessing domestic violence. Children growing up in war are exposed to repeated traumatic events. Symptoms usually appear within 3 months of the event.

PTSD can occur at any age after the first year of life and is included in DC 0–3R. DSM-5 has separate criteria for children below the age of 6, and symptoms must be assessed based on the child's age. Children can have intrusive memories and experience that the event repeats itself, including recurrent disturbing dreams with fear. They react with distress to anything reminiscent of the traumatic event, including people who talk about the event. The distress is persistent and intense, and the child finds it difficult to calm down. Affected children avoid places, things and activities, including thoughts, that remind them of the event and may exhibit selective amnesia. They can feel a great deal of shame, guilt, fear and confusion and express few positive emotions. They tend to be irritable and angry, are easily startled and may have difficulty sleeping and concentrating. They also participate less in play and other positive activities. Symptoms must have lasted for over a month.

ICD-11 includes *complex post-traumatic stress disorder*, which may develop following exposure to an event or series of events of an extremely threatening or horrific nature, most commonly prolonged or repetitive events from which escape is difficult or impossible, such as prolonged domestic violence or repeated childhood sexual or physical abuse. In addition to symptoms of PTSD, children with the complex disorder have severe and pervasive problems in affect regulation; persistent beliefs about themselves as diminished, defeated or worthless accompanied by deep and pervasive feelings of shame, guilt or failure related to the traumatic event; and persistent difficulties in sustaining relationships and in feeling close to others.

The symptoms of PTSD involve unregulated emotions and can be reminiscent of behavioral problems. Because PTSD can be mistaken for depression, it is important to look for other causes in connection with changes in behavioral patterns.

35

Addictions

Adolescence is characterized by an increase in behavioral experimentation and participation in risky behavior, such as gambling and substance abuse. Although it usually does not indicate a disorder, this kind of behavior can become more extensive and persistent in some adolescents and develop into a dependence on addictive substances such as alcohol and drugs, or gambling.

Alcohol and Substance Abuse

Problems with alcohol and other substances are most common during adulthood, but also occur in adolescence. According to DSM-5, the prevalence rate for alcohol problems lies above 4 percent among 12–17-year-olds and is higher among boys than girls. The prevalence of cannabis abuse is just over 3 percent. However, adolescents' experimentation with alcohol and drugs varies greatly between different countries. A majority of Norwegian 15–16-year-olds have tasted alcohol, but relatively few drink large amounts or consume alcohol regularly. In Denmark, consumption is significantly higher (Skretting et al., 2014).

Internet Gaming Addiction

Most children and adolescents occasionally participate in online games, and boys spend more time than girls on electronic games (Hastings et al., 2009). A significant minority spends 5 hours or more a day on computer games and Internet use. Some turn night into day and have major problems following up school work and taking part in the ordinary social life of their peer group. Accordingly, problems associated

DOI: 10.4324/9781003291275-39

with this type of addiction are quite complex. Those spending a lot of time on online games have a higher **incidence** of depression and suicide attempts than adolescents with little or moderate time use (Johansson & Götestam, 2004; Messias et al., 2011). In ICD-11, gaming disorder has two subgroups: *predominantly online* (over the Internet) and *predominantly offline*. DSM-5 lists *Internet gaming disorder* among the conditions needing more research. The difficulty of defining and delimiting these types of problem is also the reason for the lack of an accepted formal diagnosis (King et al., 2013). The DSM-5 criteria for a possible *Internet gaming disorder* are an unusual preoccupation with gaming and withdrawal symptoms in the form of irritability, anxiety and sadness when there is no access to online play. Unregulated online gaming can thus be a separate disorder as well as a symptom of other disorders.

Internet gaming addiction does not include online gambling. *Gambling disorder* is a separate diagnosis in DSM-5, and in ICD-11 *gambling disorder* also has the two subgroups, *predominantly online* and *predominantly offline*.

Internet Addiction

Recent years have seen a dramatic increase in the use of social media (see Book 7, *Social Relations, Self-awareness and Identity*, Chapter 38). Some adolescents show clear signs of *Internet addiction*, also known as *dysfunctional, pathological* or *compulsive use of the Internet*. Their thoughts are dominated by the Internet, which they use to escape negative thoughts, and they experience discomfort without online access, continuing their online activities even after having decided to stop for the day. Social media are a major contributing factor to dependency (Johansson & Götestam, 2004; van den Eijnden et al., 2011). Some users need to check social media all the time because they are afraid of being left out from something (Wallace, 2014). Neither ICD-11 nor DSM-5 include a formal diagnosis for general Internet addiction, as the nature of the addiction itself is difficult to define. Estimates vary widely, from less than 1 to over 26 percent (Kuss et al., 2013; Wallace, 2014).

Acquired Disorders

The majority of childhood and adolescent disorders are developmental, but children can also have acquired disorders. For instance near-drowning, traffic accidents and radiation treatment of brain tumors can result in neurological damage leading to various disorders (de Ruiter et al., 2013). Landau-Kleffner syndrome is a form of epilepsy that leads to infantile acquired aphasia, the loss of early language skills (Campos & de Guevara, 2007).

Progressive Disorders

Some diseases lead to dementia and loss of previously acquired skills during childhood and adolescence, including Sanfilippo syndrome and juvenile neuronal ceroid lipofuscinosis (Schoenberg & Scott, 2011).

Disorders Can Be Related

Establishing that a child meets the criteria for a given disorder is only the beginning of the diagnostic process. It is always necessary to specify a child's strengths and weaknesses, as well as the pressures and opportunities afforded by the environment. Many children have more than one disorder or symptoms resulting from several disorders, but in addition they can have their particular strong areas. It is important to avoid *diagnostic shadowing* – the use of a single diagnosis to explain all of the child's problems. Initiating treatment based on a particular diagnosis without first examining how the child functions as a whole can lead to poor developmental results.

DOI: 10.4324/9781003291275-40

Summary of Part IV

1   A *disorder* is a relatively severe reduction or deviation in develop-
    ment, learning and function within a specific area. Children may
    have *difficulties* in meeting social or academic requirements with-
    out having a disorder. Some disorders are "specific," meaning
    they are characterized by a gap between expected performance
    and actual performance. There is a seamless transition between
    ordinary difficulties and disorders.
2   The two main international classification systems are ICD and
    DSM. DC 0–3 is for children below the age of 3 years. ICF and
    ICF-CY are used to describe children's and adults' overall func-
    tioning and participation.
3   *Sensory impairments* include *visual impairment, hearing impairment*
    and *combined visual and hearing impairment.* The most common
    causes of *motor impairment* are *cerebral palsy, spina bifida* and *brain
    damage* following accidents. In addition, various diseases and syn-
    dromes can affect motor control. *Developmental motor coordination
    disorder* and *dyspraxia* affect the performance of motor actions but
    do not involve paralysis or mobility impairment.
4   *Neurodevelopmental disorders* begin early in childhood and have a
    varied course of progression clearly linked to the organism's mat-
    uration and development *as well as* to the influence of experience.
    They include *intellectual disabilities, communication* and *language dis-
    orders, autism spectrum disorders, attention deficit hyperactivity disorders,
    learning disorders,* some *motor disorders, tic disorders, schizophrenia* and
    other *psychoses.*
5   Delayed language development is common in preschool age,
    but *language disorders* can continue into school age. Children may
    have problems with different aspects of speech and language. The

prevalence of *mental disorders* is higher among children with language disorders, and vice versa.

6   The most common *learning disorders* are *reading and writing disorders (dyslexia)* and *mathematics disorders (dyscalculia)*. *Intellectual disability* influences cognitive, language, motor and social abilities. There are considerable differences between children with regard to the causes, degree and symptoms of intellectual disabilities.

7   *Autism spectrum disorder* is characterized by problems related to communication and social interaction, as well as limited, repetitive and stereotyped interests and behaviors.

8   *Attention deficit hyperactivity disorder* includes two subgroups: *predominantly hyperactivity* and *impulsivity* and *predominantly inattention*. It presents differently from childhood to adulthood, as well as in boys and in girls.

9   *Behavioral* or *externalizing disorders* include destructive, bullying, fraudulent and aggressive actions of such a scope that they become disruptive to children and adults in the environment.

10   *Internalizing disorders* include mood and anxiety disorders. *Mood disorders* include depression, mania and bipolar disorder and are among the most frequent psychological disorders among children and adolescents. Depression is relatively rare during childhood, but its prevalence increases toward adolescence. *Anxiety disorders* occur at all ages and mainly include separation anxiety, phobias, social anxiety and *generalized anxiety disorder* (GAD). Children with *selective mutism* speak only at home and with their immediate family.

11   The most characteristic feature of *obsessive-compulsive disorder* (OCD) consists of recurrent thoughts and impulses to perform specific actions, such as repeated hand washing or licking a dish. The disorder is usually accompanied by anxiety, and the individual's compulsive actions are intended to avert a situation that is perceived to be dangerous. Because they can be observed, compulsive actions are easier to identify than obsessive thoughts, which must be determined based on conversation.

12   The most common eating disorders are *anorexia*, involving undereating, and bulimia, involving binge-eating and "countermeasures" against food intake, such as intentional regurgitation or use of a laxative. Eating disorders are often accompanied by fear of obesity and negative thoughts about oneself.

13   *Reactive attachment disorder* and *disinhibited social engagement disorder* emerge in the first years of life and are related to severe neglect or

abuse. Post-traumatic stress disorder can occur at all ages and is a reaction to a stressful or traumatic event a child has experienced or learned about.

14   Although problems with alcohol and substance abuse do occur in adolescence, they are not common. Some children and adolescents show signs of *gaming disorder* related to the Internet, and some adolescents show signs of *Internet addiction*.

15   *Acquired disorders* are usually the result of injury or illness, and *progressive disorders* involve the loss of acquired skills.

Core Issues

- The use of biological and behavioral features in defining disorders.
- The differentiation of overlapping disorders.

Suggestions for Further Reading

Carr, A. (2016). *The handbook of child and adolescent clinical psychology: A contextual approach*. Hove, UK: Routledge.

Carr, A., Linehan, C., O'Reilly, G., Walsh, P. N., & McEvoy, J. (Eds) (2016). *The handbook of intellectual disability and clinical psychology practice*. Hove, UK: Routledge.

Thapar, A., Pine, D. S., Leckman, J. F., Scott, S., Snowling, M., & Taylor, E. A. (Eds) (2015). *Rutter's child and adolescent psychiatry, Sixth Edition*. Chichester, UK: Wiley.

Glossary

See subject index to find the terms in the text

Abstraction   A cognitive process that gives rise to a generalized category of something concrete, such as people, objects and events that are associated with less detailed features, aspects or similarities.

Activity   A stable and complex system of goal-oriented activities or interactions that are related to each other by theme or situation and have taken place over a long period of time.

Activity theory   The elaboration and revision of Vygotsky's *theory* by neo-Vygotskians.

Adaptation   Changes that increase the ability of a species or an individual to survive and cope with the environment.

Adaptive behavior   Behavior that enables an individual to survive and cope with the physical, social and cultural challenges of the environment.

Adaptive function   Behavioral consequences that contribute to an individual's survival.

Adolescence   The period between *childhood* and adulthood, age 1–18.

Aggression   Behavior intended to harm living beings, objects or materials.

Allele   One of several variants of the same gene at the same location on a *chromosome*, and controlling the same genetic characteristics.

Anorexia   Eating disorder involving excessive dieting, under-eating and weight loss; see *bulimia*.

Antisocial behavior   Behavior that shows little concern for other people's feelings and needs, and violates the common social and ethical norms of a culture.

Archival research   The use of psychological reports and other historical sources in research.

Assessment (in clinical work)   The mapping of an individual's strengths and weaknesses, competencies and problem areas.

Attachment   A *behavioral system* that includes various forms of *attachment behavior*; the system is activated when a child finds herself at a shorter or a longer distance from the person she is attached to, and experiences emotions such as pain, fear, stress, uncertainty or anxiety; the term is also used to describe emotional attachment to a caregiver; Attachment can be secure, insecure and disorganized; see *exploration*.

Attachment behavior   According to Bowlby, any behavior that enables a person to achieve or maintain closeness with another, clearly identified person who is perceived to be better able to cope with the environment; includes signal behavior and approach behavior.

Attention deficit disorder; ADD   Characterized by impulsivity, low ability to concentrate on a task, and little sustained attention, may experience problems with emotional regulation, motor coordination, working memory, spatial perception and executive function.

Attention deficit hyperactivity disorder; ADHD   Attention deficit disorder with restlessness and a high level of activity.

Atypical development   Course of development that differs significantly from the development of the majority of a *population*; see *individual differences* and *typical development*.

Autism spectrum disorder   Neurodevelopmental disorder that appears in the first years of life; characterized by persistent deficits in social skills, communication and language, and by repetitive behavior and restricted interests.

Autonomy   Independence, self-determination. Ability to make independent decisions related to life's everyday tasks; an important element in the formation of *identity* in *adolescence*.

Batten disease; Juvenile neuronal ceroid lipofuscinosis (JNCL)   Genetic *autosomal* recessive disease; neurodegenerative disorder with blindness at age 5–15 and development of childhood dementia with decline in cognitive and motor functions.

Behavioral disorder   All forms of behavior that are socially unacceptable in one way or another, such as running away from home, screaming, cursing, messy eating manners, bed-wetting, ritual behavior, excessive dependency, poor *emotion regulation*, *aggression*, fighting and *bullying*.

Behaviorism; Behavior analysis   Group of psychological theories that emphasize the influence of the environment to explain developmental changes.

Bulimia   Eating disorder involving binge-eating and "countermeasures" against food intake such as intentional regurgitation or use of a laxative; see *anorexia nervosa*.

Bullying   Negative actions, such as teasing and physical or verbal *aggression*, that are repeated over time and directed toward one or several individuals; direct bullying consists of open attacks on the person being bullied, while indirect bullying entails social exclusion.

Cerebral palsy   Impaired muscle function due to prenatal or early brain damage. Characterized by paralysis, poor motor or postural coordination, and increased or varying muscle tension.

Checklist   Questionnaire or interview with specific observational categories, questions or statements answered by an individual respondent or by others; often used to assess the development of an individual in one or more areas.

Childhood   Age 1–12 years.

Child-directed speech   Adults' and older children's adaptation of pitch, *intonation* and *syntax* when talking to infants and toddlers.

Classical conditioning   See *conditioning*.

Clinical Method   Piaget's term for the combined use of experimental tasks and interviews in the study of child development.

Cognition   Thinking or understanding; includes some type of perception of the world, storage in the form of mental *representation*, different ways of managing or processing new and stored experiences, and action strategies.

Cognitive structure   Complex structure of mental representations and processes that forms the basis for thoughts, actions and the perception of the outside world; evolves and changes throughout development.

Communication   Intentional conveyance of thoughts, stories, desires, ideas, emotions, etc., to one or more persons.

Concept   Mental *representation* of a category of objects, events, persons, ideas, etc.

Conditioning   The learning of a specific reaction in response to specific stimuli; includes classical and operant conditioning.

In *classical conditioning*, a neutral stimulus is associated with an unlearned or *unconditioned stimulus* that elicits an unlearned or *unconditioned response*, eventually transforming the neutral stimulus into a conditioned stimulus that elicits a conditioned response similar to the unconditioned response. In *operant conditioning*, an action is followed by an event that increases or reduces the probability that the action will be repeated under similar circumstances.

Conscience   Emotional evaluation of one's own actions, often involving feelings of having done something wrong; closely related to shame and guilt.

Conservation (in cognition)   A form of mental constancy; the ability to understand that the material or mass of an object does not change in mass, number, volume or weight unless something is taken away or added, even if external aspects of the object appear changed.

Constraint (in development)   The organism's resistance to change and adaptation to new experiences; often used in connection with the nervous system.

Constructivism   Psychological theories based on the notion that an individual constructs his or her understanding of the outside world; see *logical constructivism* and *social constructivism*.

Continuity (in development)   Development in which later ways of functioning build directly on previous functions and can be predicted based on them; see *discontinuity*.

Control group   Group of individuals that is compared with an *experimental group* as similar to the control group as possible in relevant areas, but not exposed to the experimental variable.

Core knowledge   In nativist theory, the innate abilities that form the basis for further perceptual, cognitive and linguistic development.

Correlation   Measure of the degree of covariation between two variables, ranging from −1.00 to +1.00; values close to 0.00 show a low degree of correlation; a positive correlation (+) means that a high score on one variable is associated with high score on the other; a negative cor relation (−) indicates that a high score on one variable is associated with a low score on the other.

Cortisol   Hormone that usually increases when an individual experiences stress.

Critical period   Limited time period in which an individual is especially susceptible to specific forms of positive or negative stimulation and experience; if the stimulation or experience fails to take place during this period, a similar stimulation or experience later in life will neither benefit nor harm the individual to any appreciable extent; see *sensitive period*.

Critical psychology   Theoretical tradition influenced by radical social constructivism and women's studies, as well as postmodern socology and psychoanalytic interpretation; challenges the idea that regular developmental features have a biological basis.

Cross-sectional study   Research method that traces a developmental change by comparing children at different ages; see *longitudinal study*.

Cultural tool   According to Vygotsky, a skill that has developed through generations in a culture, and that is passed on to children, such as language, the numerical system or calendar time.

Culture   The particular activities, tools, attitudes, beliefs, values, norms, etc., that characterize a group or a community.

Defense mechanism   In *psychodynamic theory*, unconscious mental strategies for dealing with inner psychological conflicts and reducing anxiety that follows the drives and impulses of the *id* and threatens control by the *ego*.

Development   Changes over time in the structure and functioning of human beings and animals as a result of interaction between biological and environmental factors.

Developmental disorder   Disorder that is congenital or appears in *infancy* or *childhood* without the presence of external injuries or similar.

Developmental pathway   One of several possible courses of development within the same area or domain.

Developmental phase   Time period central to a particular developmental process.

Developmental psychopathology   Multidisciplinary tradition among researchers and practitioners with a basis in developmental psychology; attempts to identify and influence the processes that underlie various psychological disorders, founded on assumptions about vulnerability and resilience in children, and risk and protection in the childhood environment.

Difficult temperament   According to Thomas and Chess, temperament characterized by a tendency to withdraw in new situations, general negativity, strong emotional reactions and highly irregular sleeping and eating patterns; see *easy temperament*.

Disability The difference between an individual's abilities and the demands of the environment.

Discontinuity (in development) Development in which new functions are associated with qualitative differences rather than merely a quantitative growth in previously established functions, and where the effect of past development can be altered by subsequent experiences; see *continuity, heterotypic continuity* and *homotypic continuity*.

Discriminate Distinguish between, react differentially; see *generalize*.

Dishabituation Increased response to a new stimulus or aspect of a stimulus following a reduction in response intensity due to repeated presentation of a stimulus; see *habituation*.

Domain A delimited sphere of knowledge; an area in which something is active or manifests itself.

Dynamic assessment The mapping of children's cognitive abilities by recording how much progress they make in the solution of a certain type of task after having received specific help and training for a given period; see *Learning Potential Assessment Device*.

Dynamic system (in development) A system of nonlinear *self-organizing* and *self-regulating* processes in which qualitatively new functions occur as an *integrated* result of interaction between subsystems that may have different developmental rates.

Dyslexia Severe reading and writing disorder, despite adequate sensory and intellectual abilities and appropriate training; see *learning disorder*.

Dyspraxia Partial or complete inability to perform voluntary movements.

Easy temperament According to Thomas and Chess, temperament characterized by an overall good mood, regular sleeping and eating patterns, easy adaptation to new situations, a positive attitude toward strangers, and moderate emotional reactions; easy to calm down when agitated; see *difficult temperament*.

Ecological psychology According to Bronfenbrenner, a model of child development whereby developmental conditions are determined by the complex interaction between various social systems that impact one another; see *exosystem, macrosystem, mesosystem* and *microsystem*.

Ecological validity The extent to which an observation is representative of the natural environment of the individual being observed.

Ego   In *psychoanalytic theory*, one of the three parts of the human psyche; its purpose is to regulate the drives and impulses of the *id* in relation to the realities of the world and the limitations of the *superego*.

Ego psychology   Branch of *psychodynamic psychology* that emphasizes the autonomous role of the *ego* in the development of personality, independent of drives.

Emotion   A state caused by an event important to the person and characterized by the presence of feelings; involves physiological reactions, conscious inner experience, directed action and outward expression.

Emotion regulation   Implicit and explicit strategies to adapt one's own emotional reactions and those of others in line with social and cultural conventions, especially in regard to the expression, intensity, duration and contexts in which they arise.

Empathy   Feel with someone; emotional reaction similar to the emotion another person is perceived to experience.

Enculturation   Acquisition of a culture's practices, customs, norms, values, and the like; the first foundation in this process is children's innate social orientation.

Ethology   The study of human and animal behavior under natural conditions and of the role of behavior in *evolution*. Also a branch of *evolution-based psychology*.

Evolutionary psychology; Evolution-based psychology   School of thought that focuses on the function of a particular behavior pattern during evolution, in the context of explaining human actions.

Executive functions   Cognitive functions that monitor and regulate attention and plan and supervise the execution of voluntary actions, including the inhibition to act on inappropriate impulses.

Exosystem   Subsystem of Bronfenbrenner's *bioecological model* consisting of broader social contexts that do not include the child itself, but that are important to the functioning of family and child, such as the parents' workplace and social networks, distant relatives and parents of friends; see *ecological psychology*, *macrosystem*, *mesosystem* and *microsystem*.

Experiment   Method to test a hypothesis on specific causal relationships or connections. One or several conditions are systematically altered, and the effect is recorded. As many conditions as possible are kept constant in order not to affect the outcome, increasing the probability that the results are solely related to the conditions being studied.

Experimental group   In experiments with two groups, the group that receives the experimental treatment or other influence; see *control group*.

Exploration   According to Bowlby, a behavioral system whose function is to provide information about the environment and enable the individual to better adapt to it; activated by unfamiliar and/or complex objects; deactivated once the objects have been examined and become familiar to the individual; see *attachment*.

Expressive language   The language that the child produces; see *receptive language*.

Externalizing disorder   Negative emotions directed at others; often expressed in the form of antisocial and aggressive behavior.

Field experiment   Experimental method based on modifying *independent variables* in an individual's natural environment.

Fragile X syndrome   Hereditary condition that mainly affects boys; caused by damage to the X chromosome. Characterized by the development of an elongated head, a large forehead, a high palate and a prominent chin following *puberty*. Often, but not always, entails *learning disabilities* of widely varying degree, from mild to severe, and occasionally *autism*.

Gender role; Sex role   Expectations about the actions or behavior of boys, girls, men and women in a particular society under different circumstances.

Generalize   To perceive and react in the same way to events that are similar in some respects; see *discriminate*.

Germinal period   The first 10 days of prenatal development.

Gross motor skills   Movements of the body, arms and legs.

Habituation   Gradual reduction in the intensity of a reaction or response following repeated stimulation; allows an individual to ignore familiar objects and direct attention at new ones.

Heterotypic continuity   Refers to the fact that actions differ while function remains the same at different age levels; see *continuity*, *discontinuity* and *homotypic continuity*.

Homotypic continuity   Refers to behavior that fulfills the same function at different age levels; see *continuity*, *discontinuity* and *heterotypic continuity*.

Hyperactivity   Unusually high activity level that is difficult for an individual to control.

Hyperlexia Mechanical reading ability without understanding.

Identification Process characterized by a tendency to mimic behavior and assume someone else's points of view.

Identity An individual's sense of who he or she is, as well as of affiliation with larger and smaller social groups and communities.

Imitation The deliberate execution of an action to create a correspondence between what oneself does and what someone else does; see.

Imprinting A form of rapid learning that takes place during a short and sensitive period immediately after birth; ducklings, for example, will follow the first person, animal or object they see move within a period of 48 hours after hatching.

Incidence The appearance of new occurrences of a trait, disease or similar in a particular *population* during a particular time span, often expressed as the number of incidences per 1,000 individuals per year; see *prevalence*.

Individual differences Variation in skills and characteristics between the individuals in a *population*; see *atypical development* and *typical development*.

Infancy The first year of life.

Information processing (theory) Psychological theories based on the assumption that all mental phenomena can be described and explained by models in which the flow of information is processed by one or more systems.

Inhibition Shyness and withdrawal from social challenges.

Integration (in development) Coordination; progress toward greater organization and a more complex structure.

Intellectual disability; Learning disability; Mental retardation Significant problems learning and adjusting that affect most areas of functioning; graded mild (IQ 70–50), moderate (IQ 49–35), severe (IQ 34–20) and profound (IQ below 20); in clinical contexts, a significant reduction in social adjustment is an additional criterion.

Inter-observer reliability The degree of concurrence in the scoring or assessment by two or more persons who observe the same event independent of each other, directly or on video.

Interaction (statistics) The degree of influence of one or several other variables on the relationship between an *independent* and a *dependent*.

Interaction effect An influence by one or several other factors; see *main effect* and *transaction effect*.

Internalization   Process whereby external processes are reconstructed to become internal processes, such as when children independently adopt problem-solving strategies they have previously used in interaction with others, or adopt the attitudes, characteristics and standards of others as their own.

Internalizing disorder   Negative emotions directed at oneself, anxiety, depression; often involving a negative self-image, shyness and seclusion; see *externalizing disorder*.

Irritability (temperament)   Tendency of an individual to become easily agitated and lack patience and tolerance.

Joint attention   Two or more individuals share a common focus of attention, while at the same time being aware that the same focus of attention is shared by the other person(s).

Language function   The purpose of speech; the objective one wants to achieve by conveying something to another person using language.

Learning   Relatively permanent change in understanding and behavior as the result of experience; see *development* and *maturation*.

Learning disorder   Significant problems developing skills in a specific area of knowledge, such as language impairment, reading/writing disorders (*dyslexia*) and difficulties with math (dyscalculia); often referred to as specific learning disorder as opposed to general learning disability; see *intellectual disability*.

Learning Potential Assessment Device   Test procedure to assess a child's learning abilities; tests are first performed in the traditional way, after which the child receives specific and standardized help with the tasks the child was unable to solve independently; an increase in the test score following instruction is considered a measure of the child's learning potential; see *dynamic assessment*.

Libido   Sexual or life drive; according to *psycho-analytic theory*, a source of energy aimed at reproduction, but among human beings also converted into other forms of expression. Motivates all action together with *Thanatos*.

Logical constructivism   Psychological tradition that includes Piaget's theory and the theories of others that build on it; its main principle is that children actively construct their own understanding of the outside world, and that *perception* and *cognition* are affected by logical and conceptually driven processes; see *constructivism* and *social constructivism*.

Longitudinal study   Research method that involves the observation of the same individuals at various age levels; see *cross-sectional study*.

Macrosystem   Subsystem of Bronfenbrenner's *bioecological model*; includes social institutions such as government, public services, laws, customs and values of importance to what takes place in the other systems; see *exosystem*, *mesosystem* and *microsystem*.

Main effect   An influence that is independent of other factors; see *interaction effect* and *transaction effect*.

Maturation   Developmental change caused by genetically deter-mined regulating mechanisms that are relatively independent of the individual's specific experiences; see *development* and *learning*.

Mean length of utterance (MLU)   Average number of *morphemes* per utterance; generally calculated on the basis of 100 utterances, and used to measure a child's level of language proficiency.

Mental age   See *age score*.

Mental disorder   Behavioral or psychological pattern that occurs in an individual and leads to clinically significant distress or impairment in one or more important areas of functioning.

Mental model   Subjective mind model of how the world functions and how things are connected.

Mesosystem   Subsystem of Bronfenbrenner's *bioecological model*; consists of connections between two or more microsystems a child actively participates in; see *exosystem*, *macrosystem* and *microsystem*.

Metaphor   A type of *analogy*; meaning expressed illustratively or figuratively.

Microsystem   Subsystem of Bronfenbrenner's *bioecological model* that includes the child's closest daily relationships, usually the par-ents, siblings and other relatives living with the family, preschool, school, youth clubs, neighborhood friends and the like; see *meso-system*, *exosystem* and *macrosystem*.

Mind understanding   Understanding that other people have internal states, such as knowledge, feelings and plans, that may be different from one's own and may affect their actions; see *theory of mind*.

Module (in cognition)   Isolated brain system that deals with a par-ticular type of stimulation and knowledge.

Nativism   Theoretical assumption that development proceeds according to a plan that in some way is represented genetically, and that experience has little or no effect on the developmental outcome; see *maturation*.

Naturalistic observation Research method involving the observation of an individual's regular activities in his or her ordinary environment without any attempt at outside influence.

New theory See *The new theory*.

Norm (in a test) A standard or normative score for a certain age level, based on the results from a large number of individuals.

Norm-referenced test *Test* that is *standardized* based on a representative group and scaled in such a way that the score reflects an individual's performance relative to the performance of the standardized group.

Normal distribution Statistically defined distribution around a mean; also called Gaussian curve.

Novelty preference Tendency to be more attentive to new rather than familiar stimulation; appears in infants after the age of 3 months.

Object (in psychodynamic theory) Mental representation of a person or an object that is the goal of a drive, or through which a drive can achieve its goal; see *object relation*.

Object permanence Understanding that an object continues to exist even though it cannot be perceived by the senses.

Object relation In psychodynamic theory, the dynamic interaction between an individual's mental *representations* of him or herself, and emotionally significant persons in the environment.

Observational learning Learning by observing the behavior of others and the consequences of their behavior.

Operant conditioning See *conditioning*.

Operation (cognitive) According to Piaget, the mental *representation* of actions that follow logical rules.

Oppositional defiant disorder Externalizing disorder characterized by hostility toward adults, reluctance to do what authorities say and to follow normal rules, and maliciousness and vindictiveness when met with resistance.

Orienting response Directing one's attention at a new stimulus.

Perception Knowledge gained through the senses; discernment, selection and processing of sensory input.

Personality An individual's characteristic tendency to feel, think and act in specific ways.

Personality traits Summary description of an individual's *personality*.

Pleasure principle According to *psychoanalytic theory*, one of two principles governing human functioning; seeking the immediate satisfaction of drives, needs and desires regardless of consequences; see *reality principle*.

Population (in statistics) The sum total of individuals, objects, events and the like included in a study. Also used to describe a group of individuals with a common measurable attribute, such as children in a certain school grade or young people in cities.

Preschool age Age 3–6 years.

Prevalence Relative presence of for example traits, diseases and syndromes in a particular population at a certain time; see *incidence*.

Prospective study Study that follows an individual over time; see *retrospective study*.

Protection (in development) Conditions that reduce the negative effects of *vulnerability* and *risk*.

Psychoanalytic theory Psychological theories based on Freud's theory and psychotherapeutic method (psychoanalysis); founded on the principle that an individual's thoughts and actions are determined by drives and impulses and their internal, often *unconscious*, regulation through interaction between the different parts of the human psyche; both *personality* and mental problems of children and adults are explained on the basis of unconscious processes and conflicts rooted in early childhood; see *ego*, *id*, *psychodynamic theory* and *superego*.

Psychodynamic psychology; psychodynamic theory Tradition that emphasizes the importance of feelings and needs for an individual's thoughts and actions; describes *personality* and its development based on the assumption that the human psyche involves mental forces that frequently are in conflict with each other, and have an important basis in early childhood; *psychoanalysis* belongs to this tradition.

Psychopathology Mental problems and disorders that make everyday functioning difficult.

Psychosexual phase According to *psychoanalytic theory*, a *critical period* in which a child's mental energy is directed toward a specific area of the body; the development of an individual's personality and sociocultural adaptation depends on certain stimuli and experiences and the resolution of mental conflicts during these periods.

Qualitative change   Change in the nature or quality of a phenomenon; see *quantitative change*.

Qualitative method   Research method involving the use of
descriptions and categories that need not be quantifiable, and
analyses not based on measurements and numerical processing;
does not require *replicability*, but the researcher must be able to
account for his or her standpoint and the basis for interpreting
what has been observed; see *quantitative method*.

Quantitative change   Quantifiable change in the nature or quality of a phenomenon, measurable in degree, amount, number,
and the like; see *qualitative change*.

Quantitative method   Research method involving the use of
quantifiable descriptions and categories, and analyses based on
measurements and statistical processing; requires *replicability*; see
qualitative method.

Reality principle   According to *psychoanalytic theory*, one of two
principles that govern human functioning; seeking to satisfy
drives, needs and desires in relation to what is realistic, i.e. what is
possible within a given physical, social and cultural environment;
see *pleasure principle*.

Receptive language   The language that the child understands; see
expressive language.

Reliability   Measure of how dependable a piece of information is,
and whether the observational categories and measuring methods
lead to the same result after repeated observation; see *validity*.

Replicability (in research)   Requirement that another person has
to be able to perform a study in precisely the same way it was
originally carried out, and arrive at approximately the same result.

Representation (mental)   An individual's mental storage of
understanding and knowledge about the world.

Representative sample   A group of individuals with the same
distribution of relevant characteristics as the *population* represented
by the sample, so that the results of the sample can be assumed to
be valid for the entire population.

Resilience   Attributes that lead to a positive development under
difficult childhood conditions, such as children who are biologically or socially at *risk* of aberrant or delayed development; see
vulnerability.

Retrospective study   Study in which an individual is asked about
earlier events.

Rett syndrome   Genetic syndrome that almost exclusively affects girls; characterized by severe *intellectual disability* and motor and language impairment; development is often normal for the first 6–18 months of life, with a consequent decline in functioning. Believed to be mainly caused by a defective control gene (MeCP2) on the X chromosome that fails to switch off other X chromosome genes at the right time.

Risk   Increased likelihood of a negative developmental outcome; may be linked to biological and environmental factors.

Schema   Mental *representation* that emerges when actions are generalized by means of repetition and transformed through mental processing, thus shaping the individual's perception of the environment; see *cognitive structure*.

School age   Age 6–12.

Self   Personal awareness, perception or evaluation of oneself.

Self-efficacy   The experience of acting and having control over one's own life; belief in one's own ability to deal with different situations and events.

Self-esteem   The assessment of one's own characteristics in relation to an inner standard that includes how and who one wishes to be; can also refer to questionnaires, surveys and the like about a person's characteristics.

Self-image   Positive or negative perception of oneself and one's own characteristics.

Self-regulation   The ability to monitor and adapt one's own thoughts, feelings, reactions and actions in order to cope with the requirements, challenges and opportunities of the environment and be able to achieve one's goals; also referred to as self-control.

Sensitive period   Limited period of time when an individual is particularly susceptible to specific forms of positive or negative stimulation and experience; if the stimulation or experience does not take place during the given time period, the individual will still be able to take advantage of, or be impaired by, similar types of stimulation or experience later in life, but to a lesser extent; see *critical period*.

Sensitivity (of a caregiver)   Ability to understand a child's condition, respond quickly and adequately to the child's *signals* and behavior, and provide challenges the child is able to master.

Shaping (of behavior)   Step-by-step *reinforcement* of behavior in such a way that it gradually changes and increasingly resembles desired behavior; part of *operant conditioning*.

Sign language   Visual-manual language, primarily using movements of the arms, hands and fingers, supported by body movements, mouth movements and facial gestures.

Sociability (temperament)   Interest and enjoyment in being in the company of other people.

Social constructivism   Psychological theories based on the notion that children construct their understanding of the outside world through interaction and cooperation with other people, and that people in different cultures (including the subcultures of a society) can perceive one and the same phenomenon in different ways; see *logical constructivism*.

Social learning theory   See *cognitive behavior theory*.

Social referencing   Using other people's emotional reactions to evaluate uncertain situations; see *emotion regulation*.

Socioeconomic status (SES)   Assessment of an individual's economic and social status in society; for children, usually based on information about the parents' education and occupation.

Stability (in development)   Describes the constancy of an individual's position in relation to peers with respect to a particular characteristic; the fact that individual differences in the execution of a skill are constant from one developmental stage to another.

Stage (in development)   Delimited period of time in which thoughts, feelings and behavior are organized in a way that is qualitatively different from the preceding or following periods.

Stage theory   Theory based on the assumption that development proceeds in distinct and qualitatively different *stages*.

Standard deviation   Measure of the spread of *quantitative* data; indicates the average degree of deviation in the score or numerical value of a variable from the total average; see *normal distribution*.

Strange Situation   Standardized situation to assess the quality of attachment between an adult and a child aged 1–2 years; see *attachment*.

Superego   In *psychoanalytic theory*, one of the three parts of the human psyche, consisting of internalized demands and expectations, primarily from parents, but also from other important persons in the child's environment; its function is to ensure that an individual's actions remain within the norms and values of culture; see *id* and *ego*.

Symbol   Something that represents something other than itself, such as a sign, a word, an image or the like.

Synapse   Contact point between the *axon* of a nerve cell and the body of another nerve cell via its *dendrites*; this is where the transmission of impulses occurs.

Syndrome   Set of attributes and behavioral characteristics that regularly occur together.

Temperament   A biologically determined pattern of emotional reactivity and regulation unique to an individual; includes the degree of *emotionality*, *irritability* and *activity level*, and reactions to and ability to cope with emotional situations, new impressions and changes; see *easy temperament* and *difficult temperament*.

Test   Measurement instrument; a collection of questions or tasks that provide a basis for assessing an individual's performance relative to peers or a specific set of criteria; see *norm-referenced test*.

Thanatos   According to *psychoanalytic theory*, the aggressive and destructive drive that together with *libido* motivates all human action.

The new theory   A common term for Piaget's final revision of his theory of cognitive development, which makes allowances for some of the criticism directed at *the standard theory*, in particular issues concerning Piaget's assumptions on *domain-general* development.

The standard theory   A common term for Piaget's theory of cognitive development as it appeared in its basic form in the 1950s and 1960s; see *the new theory*.

Theory of mind   The understanding that human beings are thinking and sentient beings who act according to how they perceive a given situation; see *mind understanding*.

Transaction effect   The result of reciprocal influences between an individual and the environment over time, see *main effect* and *interaction effect*.

Transactional model   Developmental model based on mutual interaction between an individual and the environment over time: the environment changes the individual, the individual changes the environment, which in turn changes the individual, and so on.

Typical development   Course of development that characterizes the majority of a *population*; see *atypical development* and *individual differences*.

Unconscious   Not within the sphere of conscious attention; in *psychoanalytic theory*, an inaccessible part of consciousness where repressed, often anxiety-eliciting memories and desires are stored.

Universality   General validity; phenomena that exist in all cultures, such as language.

Validity   The soundness or factual accuracy of knowledge; whether a given method measures what it aims to measure and whether the results provide answers to the research questions posed.

Vulnerability   An individual's susceptibility to be adversely affected by particular conditions or circumstances in the environment; see *resilience* and *risk*.

Working memory   Part of the memory system related to what an individual does while trying to remember something for a short period of time or dealing with a problem. Characterized by limited storage and processing capacity, and a rapid reduction in content if not repeated.

Working model (in social relations)   Mental representation of an early relationship that forms the basis for expectations about the nature of social relationships, such as a caregiver's inclination to provide emotional support and be devoted and reliable.

Zone of proximal development   Children's mastery of skills in collaboration with more competent individuals within a specific area of knowledge or expertise, as opposed to self-mastery.

Bibliography

Achenbach, T. M., & Rescorla, L. A. (2000). *Manual for the ASEBA preschool forms and profiles: An integrated system of multi-informant assessment.* Burlington, VT: University of Vermont Department of Psychiatry.

Achenbach, T. M., & Rescorla, L. A. (2001). *Manual for the ASEBA school-age forms and profiles.* Burlington, VT: Research Center for Children, Youth, and Families, University of Vermont.

Adrian, M., Lyon, A. R., Oti, R., & Tininenko, J. (2010). Developmental foundations and clinical applications of social information processing: A review. *Marriage and Family Review, 46,* 327–345.

Akhutina, T. V. (2003). L. S. Vygotsky and A. R. Luria: Foundations of neuropsychology. *Journal of Russian and East European Psychology, 41,* 159–190.

Algozzine, B., Porfeli, E., Wang, C., McColl, A., & Audette, R. (2012). Achievement gaps: Learning disabilities, community capital, and school composition. In W. Sittiprapaporn (Ed.), *Learning disabilities* (pp. 19–30). Rijeka, Croatia: InTech.

American Psychiatric Association (2013). *Diagnostic and statistical manual of mental disorders, Fifth edition (DSM-5).* Washington, DC: American Psychiatric Association.

Anderson, D. I., Campos, J. J., Witherington, D. C., Dahl, A., Rivera, M., He, M., Uchiyama, I., & Barbu-Roth, M. (2013). The role of locomotion in psychological development. *Frontiers in Psychology, 4,* 440.

Anholt, G. E., Aderka, I. M., van Balkom, A. J. L. M., Smit, J. H., Schruers, K., van der Wee, N. J. A., Eikelenboom, M., De Luca, V., & van Oppen, P. (2014). Age of onset in obsessive–compulsive disorder: Admixture analysis with a large sample. *Psychological Medicine, 44,* 185–194.

Åsberg, J., Carlsson, M., Oderstam, A. M., & Miniscalco, C. (2010). Reading comprehension among typically developing Swedish-speaking 10–12-year-olds: Examining subgroups differentiated in terms of language and decoding skills. *Logopedics Phoniatrics Vocology, 35,* 189–193.

Asendorpf, J. B., Conner, M., De Fruyt, F., De Houwer, J., Denissen, J. J., Fiedler, K., Fiedler, S., Funder, D. C., Kliegl, R., Nosek, B. A., et al. (2013). Recommendations for increasing replicability in psychology. *European Journal of Personality, 27,* 108–119.

Ashiabi, G. S., & O'Neal, K. K. (2015). Child social development in context: An examination of some propositions in Bronfenbrenner's bioecological theory. *SAGE Open, 5,* 1–14.

Aslin, R. N. (2007). What's in a look? *Developmental Science, 10,* 48–53.

Baillargeon, R. (1987). Young infants' reasoning about the physical and spatial properties of a hidden object. *Cognitive Development, 2,* 179–200.

Baillargeon, R., Kotovsky, L., & Needham, A. (1995). The acquisition of physical knowledge in infancy. In D. Sperber, D. Premack & A. J. Premack (Eds), *Causal cognition* (pp. 79–116). Oxford: Oxford University Press.

Bakermans-Kranenburg, M. J., & van IJzendoorn, M. H. (2006). Gene-environment interaction of the dopamine D4 receptor (DRD4) and observed maternal insensitivity predicting externalizing behavior in preschoolers. *Developmental Psychobiology, 48,* 406–409.

Baldry, A. C. (2003). Bullying in schools and exposure to domestic violence. *Child Abuse and Neglect, 27,* 713–732.

Bandura, A. (1978). The self system in reciprocal determinism. *American Psychologist, 33,* 344–358.

Bandura, A. (1986). *Social foundations of thought and action: A social cognitive theory.* Upper Saddle River, NJ: Prentice Hall.

Bandura, A. (2001). Social cognitive theory: An agentic perspective. *Annual Review of Psychology, 52,* 1–26.

Bandura, A. (2006). Toward a psychology of human agency. *Perspectives on Psychological Science, 1,* 164–180.

Barrett, H. C., & Kurzban, R. (2006). Modularity in cognition: Framing the debate. *Psychological Review, 113,* 628.

Barton, E. E. (2010). Development of a taxonomy of pretend play for children with disabilities. *Infants and Young Children, 23,* 247–261.

Bates, E., Bretherton, I., & Snyder, L. (1988). *From first words to grammar. Individual differences and dissociable mechanisms.* Cambridge: Cambridge University Press.

Bates, E., Elman, J., Johnson, M. H., Karmiloff-Smith, A., Parisi, D., & Plunkett, K. (1998). Innateness and emergentism. In W. Bechtel & G. Graham (Eds), *A companion to cognitive science* (pp. 590–601). Oxford: Basil Blackwell.

Beilin, H. (1992). Piaget's new theory. In H. Beilin & P. B. Pufall (Eds), *Piaget's theory: Prospects and possibilities* (pp. 1–17). Hillsdale, NJ: Erlbaum.

Bell, R. Q. (1968). A reinterpretation of the direction of effects in studies of socialization. *Psychological Review, 75,* 81–95.

Benson, M. J., & Buehler, C. (2012). Family process and peer deviance influences on adolescent aggression: Longitudinal effects across early and middle adolescence. *Child Development, 83,* 1213–1228.

Bergman, L. R., Corovic, J., Ferrer-Wreder, L., & Modig, K. (2014). High IQ in early adolescence and career success in adulthood: Findings from a Swedish longitudinal study. *Research in Human Development, 11*, 165–185.

Bergman, R. L., Piacentini, J., & McCracken, J. T. (2002). Prevalence and description of selective mutism in a school-based sample. *Journal of the American Academy of Child and Adolescent Psychiatry, 41*, 938–946.

Berninger, V. W. (2015). *Interdisciplinary frameworks for schools: Best professional practices for serving the needs of all students.* Washington, DC: American Psychological Association.

Beuker, K. T., Schjølberg, S., Lie, K. K., Swinkels, S., Rommelse, N. N., & Buitelaar, J. K. (2014). ESAT and M-CHAT as screening instruments for autism spectrum disorders at 18 months in the general population: Issues of overlap and association with clinical referrals. *European Child and Adolescent Psychiatry, 23*, 1081–1091.

Biederman, J. (2005). Attention-deficit/hyperactivity disorder: A selective overview. *Biological Psychiatry, 57*, 1215–1220.

Biggerstaff, D. (2012). Qualitative research methods in psychology. In G. Rossi (Ed.), *Psychology – selected papers* (pp. 175–206). Croatia: InTech Open Science.

Bijou, S. W. (1968). Ages, stages, and the naturalization of human development. *American Psychologist, 23*, 419–427.

Bijou, S. W., & Baer, D. M. (1961). *Child development, Volume 1: A systematic and empirical theory.* New York, NY: Appleton-Century-Crofts.

Binet, A., & Simon, T. (1905). Méthodes nouvelles pour diagnostic du niveau intéllectuel des abnormaux. *L'Année Psychologique, 11*, 191–244.

Bishop, D. V. M. (2006). What causes specific language impairment in children? *Current Directions in Psychological Science, 15*, 217–221.

Bishop, D. V. M. (2007). Using mismatch negativity to study central auditory processing in developmental language and literacy impairments: Where are we, and where should we be going? *Psychological Bulletin, 133*, 651–672.

Bishop, D. V. M., & Snowling, M. J. (2004). Developmental dyslexia and specific language impairment: Same or different? *Psychological Bulletin, 130*, 858–886.

Bitner-Glindzicz, M., & Saihan, Z. (2013). Usher syndrome. In T. D. Kenny & P. L. Beales (Eds), *Ciliopathies: A reference for clinicians* (pp. 238–261). Oxford: Oxford University Press.

Björck-Åkesson, E., Wilder, J., Granlund, M., Pless, M., Simeonsson, R., Adolfsson, M., Almqvist, L., Augustine, L., Klang, N., & Lillvist, A. (2010). The International Classification of Functioning, Disability and Health and the version for children and youth as a tool in child habilitation/early childhood intervention – Feasibility and usefulness as a common language and frame for practice. *Disability and Rehabilitation, 32*, 125–138.

Bjorklund, D. F., & Pellegrini, A. D. (2002). *The origins of human nature: Evolutionary developmental psychology.* Washington, DC: American Psychological Association.

Blair, E. (2010). Epidemiology of the cerebral palsies. *Orthopedic Clinics of North America*, *41*, 441–455.

Block, J., & Block, J. H. (2006). Venturing a 30-year longitudinal study. *American Psychologist*, *61*, 315–327.

Blowers, G., Cheung, B. T., & Ru, H. (2009). Emulation vs. indigenization in the reception of Western psychology in Republican China: An analysis of the content of Chinese psychology journals (1922–1937). *Journal of the History of the Behavioral Sciences*, *45*, 21–33.

Bond, E. (2010). Managing mobile relationships: Children's perceptions of the impact of the mobile phone on relationships in their everyday lives. *Childhood*, *17*, 514–529.

Boorsboom, D., Mellenbergh, G. J., & van Heerden, J. (2004). The concept of validity. *Psychological Review*, *111*, 1061–1071.

Bornstein, M. H. (Ed.) (2010). *Handbook of cultural developmental science*. Hove, UK: Psychology Press.

Bowlby, J. (1969). *Attachment and loss, Volume 1. Attachment*. Harmondsworth, UK: Penguin.

Bowlby, J. (1973). *Attachment and loss, Volume 2. Separation: Anxiety and anger*. Harmondsworth, UK: Penguin.

Bowlby, J. (1980). *Attachment and Loss: Volume 3. Loss: Sadness and depression*. New York, NY: Basic Books.

Brem, S., Grünblatt, E., Drechsler, R., Riederer, P., & Walitza, S. (2014). The neurobiological link between OCD and ADHD. *ADHD Attention Deficit and Hyperactivity Disorders*, *6*, 175–202.

Bronfenbrenner, U. (1979). *The ecology of human development*. Cambridge, MA: Harvard University Press.

Bronfenbrenner, U., & Morris, P. A. (2006). The bioecological model of human developmental. In W. Damon & R. M. Lerner (Eds), *Handbook of child psychology, Sixth edition, Volume 1: Theoretical models of human development* (pp. 793–828). New York, NY: John Wiley.

Brown, R. (1973). *A first language*. Cambridge, MA: Harvard University Press.

Brummelman, E., Thomaes, S., Overbeek, G., Orobio de Castro, B., van den Hout, M. A., & Bushman, B. J. (2014). "That's not just beautiful – that's incredibly beautiful!" the adverse impact of inflated praise on children with low self-esteem. *Psychological Science*, *25*, 728–735.

Bühler, C. (1928). *Kindheit und Jugend: Genese des Bewusstseins*. Leipzig: Hirzel.

Burman, E. (2001). Beyond the baby and the bathwater: Postdualistic developmental psychologies for diverse childhoods. *European Early Childhood Education Research Journal*, *9*, 5–22.

Burman, E. (2008). *Developments: Child, image, nation*. Abingdon, UK: Routledge.

Burman, E. (2013a). Conceptual resources for questioning "child as educator". *Studies in Philosophy and Education*, *32*, 229–243.

Burman, E. (2013b). Desiring development? Psychoanalytic contributions to antidevelopmental psychology. *International Journal of Qualitative Studies in Education, 26*, 56–74.

Burman, E. (2017). *Deconstructing developmental psychology, Third edition.* Abingdon, UK: Routledge.

Burton, T. D. (1994). *Introduction to dynamic systems analysis.* New York, NY: McGraw-Hill.

Bush, N. R., & Boyce, W. T. (2014). The contributions of early experience to biological development and sensitivity to context. In M. Lewis and K. Rudolph (Eds), *Handbook of developmental psychopathology* (pp. 287–309). New York, NY: Springer.

Buss, D. M., & Duntley, J. D. (2011). The evolution of intimate partner violence. *Aggression and Violent Behavior, 16*, 411–419.

Buss, D. M., & Penke, L. (2015). Evolutionary personality psychology. In M. Mikulincer, P. R. Shaver, M. L. Cooper, & R. J. Larsen (Eds), *APA handbook of personality and social psychology, Volume 4: Personality processes and individual differences* (pp. 3–29). Washington, DC: American Psychological Association.

Butterworth, B. (2008). Developmental dyscalculia. In J. Reed & J. Warner-Rogers (Eds), *Child Neuropsychology* (pp. 274–357). Oxford: Blackwell.

Callaghan, J., Andenæs, A., & Macleod, C. (2015). Deconstructing developmental psychology 20 years on: Reflections, implications and empirical work. *Feminism and Psychology, 25*, 255–265.

Campos, J. G., & de Guevara, L. G. (2007). Landau-Kleffner syndrome. *Journal of Pediatric Neurology, 5*, 93–99.

Campos, J. J., Anderson, D. I., Barbu-Roth, M. A., Hubbard, E. M., Hertenstein, M. J., & Witherington, D. (2000). Travel broadens the mind. *Infancy, 1*, 149–219.

Campos, J. J., Witherington, D., Anderson, D. I., Frankel, C. I., Uchiyama, I., & Barbu-Roth, M. (2008). Rediscovering development in infancy. *Child Development, 79*, 1625–1632.

Cardoos, S. L., & Hinshaw, S. P. (2011). Friendship as protection from peer victimization for girls with and without ADHD. *Journal of Abnormal Child Psychology, 39*, 1035–1045.

Carey, S. (2011). Précis of the origin of concepts. *Behavioral and Brain Sciences, 34*, 113–124.

Carlier, M., & Roubertoux, P. L. (2014). Genetic and environmental influences on intellectual disability in childhood. In D. Finkel & C. A. Reynold (Eds), *Behavior genetics of cognition across the lifespan* (pp. 69–101). New York, NY: Springer.

Carpendale, J. I. M., & Carpendale, A. B. (2010). The development of pointing: From personal directedness to interpersonal direction. *Human Development, 53*, 110–126.

Carr, A. (2016). *The handbook of child and adolescent clinical psychology: A contextual approach.* Hove, UK: Routledge.

Carr, A., & O'Reilly, G. (2016a). Diagnosis, classification and epidemiology. In A. Carr, G. O'Reilly, P. N. Walsh & J. McEvoy (Eds), *The handbook of intellectual disability and clinical psychology practice* (pp. 3–44). Hove, UK: Routledge.

Carr, A., Linehan, C., O'Reilly, G., Walsh, P. N., & McEvoy, J. (Eds) (2016). *The handbook of intellectual disability and clinical psychology practice.* Hove, UK: Routledge.

Carruthers, P. (2006). *The architecture of the mind: Massive modularity and the flexibility of thought.* Oxford: Oxford University Press.

Carruthers, P. (2008). Précis of the architecture of the mind: Massive modularity and the flexibility of thought. *Mind and Language, 23,* 257–262.

Case, R. (1985). *Intellectual development: Birth to adulthood.* London: Academic Press.

Caspi, A., Houts, R. M., Belsky, D. W., Harrington, H., Hogan, S., Ramrakha, S., Poulton, R., & Moffitt, T. E. (2016). Childhood forecasting of a small segment of the population with large economic burden. *Nature Human Behaviour, 1,* 0005.

Chaiklin, S. (2003). The zone of proximal development in Vygotsky's analysis of learning and instruction. In A. Kozulin, B. Gindis, V. Ageyev & S. Miller (Eds), *Vygotsky's educational theory in cultural context* (pp. 39–64). Cambridge: Cambridge University Press.

Chi, M. T. H. (1978). Knowledge structures and memory development. In R. S. Siegler (Ed.), *Children's thinking: What develops?* (pp. 73–96). Hillsdale, NJ: Lawrence Erlbaum.

Chomsky, N. (2000). *New horizons in the study of language and mind.* Cambridge: Cambridge University Press.

Cicchetti, D. (2013). Annual research review: Resilient functioning in maltreated children–past, present, and future perspectives. *Journal of Child Psychology and Psychiatry, 54 (4),* 402–422.

Cicchetti, D., & Toth, S. L. (2009). The past achievements and future promises of developmental psychopathology: The coming of age of a discipline. *Journal of Child Psychology and Psychiatry, 50,* 16–25.

Clark, I. (2012). Formative assessment: Assessment is for self-regulated learning. *Educational Psychology Review, 24,* 205–249.

Cline, T., & Baldwin, S. (2004). *Selective mutism in children, Second edition.* London: Whurr/Wiley.

Clinton, D. (2010). Towards an ecology of eating disorders: Creating sustainability through the integration of scientific research and clinical practice. *European Eating Disorders Review, 18,* 1–9.

Coleman, P. K., & Karraker, K. H. (1998). Self-efficacy and parenting quality: Findings and future applications. *Developmental Review, 18,* 47–85.

Conti-Ramsden, G., Simkin, Z., & Botting, N. (2006). The prevalence of autistic spectrum disorders in adolescents with a history of specific language impairment (SLI). *Journal of Child Psychology and Psychiatry, 47,* 621–628.

Cook, T. D., & Campbell, D. T. (1979). *Quasi-experimentation: Design and analysis for field settings*. Boston, MA: Houghton Mifflin.

Cordier, R., Munro, N., Speyer, R., Wilkes-Gillan, S., & Pearce, W. (2014). Reliability and validity of the Pragmatics Observational Measure (POM): A new observational measure of pragmatic language for children. *Research in Developmental Disabilities, 35*, 1588–1598.

Cormier, E. (2008). Attention deficit/hyperactivity disorder: A review and update. *Journal of Pediatric Nursing, 23*, 345–357.

Cosmides, L., & Tooby, J. (1994). Origins of domain specificity: The evolution of functional organization. In L. Hirschfeld & S. Gelman (Eds), *Mapping the mind: Domain-specificity in cognition and culture* (pp. 85–116). New York, NY: Cambridge University Press.

Cox, M. J., Mills-Koonce, R., Propper, C., & Gariépy, J. L. (2010). Systems theory and cascades in developmental psychopathology. *Development and Psychopathology, 22*, 497–506.

Cozby, P. C. (1993). *Methods in behavioral research, Fifth edition*. London: Mayfield.

Creswell, J. W., & Miller, D. L. (2000). Determining validity in qualitative inquiry. *Theory into Practice, 39*, 124–130.

Crick, N. R., & Dodge, K. A. (1994). A review and reformulation of social information-processing mechanisms in children's social adjustment. *Psychological Bulletin, 115*, 74–101.

Cummings, L. (2008). *Clinical linguistics*. Edinburgh: Edinburgh University Press.

Cummings, L. (2014). *Pragmatic disorders*. Dordrecht: Springer.

Dahl, A., Schuck, R. K., & Campos, J. J. (2013). Do young toddlers act on their social preferences? *Developmental Psychology, 49*, 1964–1970.

Dale, N., & Edwards, L. (2015). Children with specific sensory impairments. In A. Thapar, D. S. Pine, J. F. Leckman, S. Scott, M. J. Snowling & E. Taylor (Eds), *Rutter's child and adolescent psychiatry, Sixth edition* (pp. 612–622). Chichester, UK: Wiley.

Dale, P. S., & Goodman, J. C. (2005). Commonality and individual differences in vocabulary growth. In M. Tomasello & D. I. Slobin (Eds), *Beyond naturenurture: Essays in honor of Elizabeth Bates* (pp. 41–78). Mahwah, NJ: Erlbaum.

Dammeyer, J. (2010). Prevalence and aetiology of congenitally deafblind people in Denmark. *International Journal of Audiology, 49*, 76–82.

Dammeyer, J. (2014). Deafblindness: A review of the literature. *Scandinavian Journal of Public Health, 42*, 554–562.

Darwin, C. (1877). A biographical sketch of an infant. *Mind, 2*, 285–294.

Davies, J., & Wright, J. (2008). Children's voices: A review of the literature pertinent to looked-after children's views of mental health services. *Child and Adolescent Mental Health, 13*, 26–31.

De Los Reyes, A., & Kazdin, A. E. (2005). Informant discrepancies in the assessment of childhood psychopathology: A critical review, theoretical framework, and recommendations for further study. *Psychological Bulletin, 131*, 483–509.

De Ruiter, M. A., Van Mourik, R., Schouten-van Meeteren, A. Y., Grooten-huis, M. A., & Oosterlaan, J. (2013). Neurocognitive consequences of a pae-diatric brain tumour and its treatment: A meta-analysis. *Developmental Medicine and Child Neurology, 55*, 408–417.

Dekker, T. M., & Karmiloff-Smith, A. (2011). The dynamics of ontogeny: A neuroconstructivist perspective on genes, brains, cognition and behavior. *Progress in Brain Research, 189*, 23–33.

Demetriou, A., Spanoudis, G., & Mouyi, A. (2011). Educating the developing mind: Towards an overarching paradigm. *Educational Psychology Review, 23*, 601–663.

Dennis, M., Landry, S. H., Barnes, M., & Fletcher, J. M. (2006). A model of neu-rocognitive function in spina bifida over the life span. *Journal of the International Neuropsychological Society, 12*, 285–296.

DeVries, R. (2000). Vygotsky, Piaget, and education: A reciprocal assimilation of theories and educational practices. *New Ideas in Psychology, 18*, 187–213.

Dietz, A., Löppönen, T., Valtonen, H., Hyvärinen, A., & Löppönen, H. (2009). Prevalence and etiology of congenital or early acquired hearing impairment in Eastern Finland. *International Journal of Pediatric Otorhinolaryngology, 73*, 1353–1357.

Dromi, E. (1993). The mysteries of early lexical development: Underlying cogni-tive and linguistic processes in meaning acquisition. In E. Dromi (Ed.), *Lan-guage and cognition: A developmental perspective* (pp. 32–60). Norwood, NJ: Ablex.

Durrant, R., & Ward, T. (2012). The role of evolutionary explanations in crimi-nology. *Journal of Theoretical and Philosophical Criminology, 4*, 1–37.

Eder, D., & Fingerson, L. (2001). Interviewing children and adolescents. In A. Holstein & J. F. Gubrium (Eds), *Inside interviewing: New lenses, new concerns* (pp. 33–53). Thousand Oaks, CA: Sage.

Elman, J. L., Bates, E. A., Johnson, M. H., Karmiloff-Smith, A., Parisi, D., & Plunkett, K. (1996). *Rethinking innateness. A connectionist perspective on develop-ment*. London: MIT Press.

Emde, R. N. (1998). Early emotional development: New modes of thinking for research and intervention. *Pediatrics, 102* (Supplement *E1*), 1236–1243.

Emery, A. E., Muntoni, F., & Quinlivan, R. C. (2015). *Duchenne muscular dystro-phy, Fourth edition*. Oxford: Oxford University Press.

Erikson, E. H. (1963). *Childhood and society*. London: Norton.

Erola, J., Jalonen, S., & Lehti, H. (2016). Parental education, class and income over early life course and children's achievement. *Research in Social Stratification and Mobility, 44*, 33–43.

Fagan, J. F., & Detterman, D. K. (1992). The Fagan Test of Infant Intelli-gence: A technical summary. *Journal of Applied Developmental Psychology, 13*, 173–193.

Fairbairn, W. R. D. (1952). *Psychoanalytic studies of the personality*. London: Rout-ledge and Kegan Paul.

Fantz, R. L. (1956). A method for studying early visual development. *Perceptual and Motor Skills, 6,* 13–15.

Fantz, R. L. (1958). Pattern vision in young infants. *Psychological Record, 8,* 43–47.

Fantz, R. L. (1961). The origin of form perception. *Scientific American, 204,* 66–72.

Fazzi, E., Signorini, S. G., La Piana, R., Bertone, C., Misefari, W., Galli, J., Balottinm U., & Bianchi, P. E. (2012). Neuro-ophthalmological disorders in cerebral palsy: Ophthalmological, oculomotor, and visual aspects. *Developmental Medicine and Child Neurology, 54,* 730–736.

Fekkes, M., Pijpers, F. I., & Verloove-Vanhorick, S. P. (2005). Bullying: Who does what, when and where? Involvement of children, teachers and parents in bullying behavior. *Health Education Research, 20,* 81–91.

Feldman, D., Banerjee, A., & Sur, M. (2016). Developmental dynamics of Rett syndrome. *Neural Plasticity, 2016,* 6154080.

Feuerstein, R., Feuerstein, R., & Gross, S. (1997). The Learning Potential Assessment Device. In D. P. Flanagan, J. L. Genshaft & P. L. Harrison (Eds), *Contemporary intellectual assessment* (pp. 297–313). London: Guilford Press.

Fintoft, K., Bollingmo, M., Feilberg, J., Gjettum B., & Mjaavatn, P. E. (1983). *Fire år: En undersøkelse av normalspråket hos norske 4-åringer.* Trondheim: Universitetet i Trondheim.

Fischer, K. W. (1980). A theory of cognitive development: The control and construction of hierarchies of skills. *Psychological Review, 87,* 477–531.

Fischer, K. W., & Connell, M. W. (2003). Two motivational systems that shape development: Epistemic and self-organizing. *British Journal of Educational Psychology: Monograph Series II, 2,* 103–123.

Fischer, K. W., Shaver, P. R., & Carnochan, P. (1990). How emotions develop and how they organise development. *Cognition and Emotion, 4,* 81–127.

Fitzgerald, J., & Pavuluri, M. (2015). Bipolar disorder. In T. P. Gullotta, R. W. Plant & M. A. Evans (Eds), *Handbook of adolescent behavioral problems* (pp. 193–208). New York, NY: Springer.

Flanigan, K. M. (2012). The muscular dystrophies. *Seminars in Neurology, 32,* 255–263.

Floyd, R. G. (2010). Assessment of cognitive abilities and cognitive processes: Issues, applications and fit with a problem-solving model. In G. G. Pedacock, R. A. Ervin, E. J. Daly & K. W. Merrell (Eds), *Practical handbook of school psychology: Effective practices for the 21st century* (pp. 48–66). New York, NY: Guilford Press.

Flynn, J. R. (2007). *What is intelligence? Beyond the Flynn effect.* Cambridge: Cambridge University Press.

Fontaine, R. G. (2010). New developments in developmental research on social information processing and antisocial behavior. *Journal of Abnormal Child Psychology, 38,* 569–573.

Forte, L. A., Timmer, S., & Urquiza, A. (2014). A brief history of evidence-based practice. In S. Timmer & A. Urquiza (Eds), *Evidence-based approaches for the treatment of maltreated children* (pp. 13–18). New York, NY: Springer.

Fox, L., Carta, J. J., Strain, P. S., Dunlap, G., & Hemmeter, M. L. (2010). Response to intervention and the Pyramid Model. *Infants and Young Children*, *23*, 3–13.

Fraiberg, S. (1977). *Insights from the blind*. New York, NY: Basic Books.

Frances, A. J., & Nardo, J. M. (2013). ICD-11 should not repeat the mistakes made by DSM-5. *British Journal of Psychiatry*, *203*, 1–2.

Freud, A. (1966). *Normality and pathology in childhood*. London: Hogarth Press.

Freud, S. (1894). The neuro-psychoses of defence. In *The standard edition of the complete works of Sigmund Freud* (pp. 43–61). London: Hogarth Press.

Freud, S. (1905). *Three essays on the theory of sexuality*. London: Allen and Unwin.

Freud, S. (1911). Two principles in mental functioning. In *The standard edition of the complete works of Sigmund Freud, Volume 12* (pp. 213–226), London: Hogarth Press.

Freud, S. (1916). *A general introduction to psychoanalysis*. New York, NY: Liveright.

Freud, S. (1927). *The ego and the id*. London: Hogarth Press.

Freud, S. (1930). *Civilization and its discontents*. Oxford: Hogarth Press.

Frick, P. J., & Nigg, J. T. (2012). Current issues in the diagnosis of attention deficit hyperactivity disorder, oppositional defiant disorder, and conduct disorder. *Annual Review of Clinical Psychology*, *8*, 77–107.

Garber, J., & Rao, U. (2014). Depression in children and adolescents. In M. Lewis & K. D. Rudolph (Eds), *Handbook of developmental psychopathology, Third edition* (pp. 489–520).

Garmezy, N. (1991). Resiliency and vulnerability to adverse developmental outcomes associated with poverty. *American Behavioral Scientist*, *34*, 416–430.

Geddie, B. E., Bina, M. J., Miller, M. M., Bathshaw, M. L., Roizen, N. J., & Lotrecchiano, G. R. (2013). Vision and visual impairment. In G. Lotrecchiano, N. Roizen & M. Batshaw (Eds), *Children with disabilities, Seventh edition* (pp. 169–188). Baltimore, MD: Brookes.

Gershoff, E. T., Lansford, J. E., Sexton, H. R., Davis-Kean, P., & Sameroff, A. J. (2012). Longitudinal links between spanking and children's externalizing behaviors in a national sample of White, Black, Hispanic, and Asian American families. *Child Development*, *83*, 838–843.

Gibbs, J., Appleton, J., & Appleton, R. (2007a). Dyspraxia or developmental coordination disorder? Unravelling the enigma. *Archives of Disease in Childhood*, *92*, 534–539.

Gifford, S., & Rockliffe, F. (2012). Mathematics difficulties: Does one approach fit all? *Research in Mathematics Education*, *14*, 1–15.

Golden, S. D., McLeroy, K. R., Green, L. W., Earp, J. A., & Lieberman, L. D. (2015). Upending the social ecological model to guide health promotion efforts toward policy and environmental change. *Health Education and Behavior*, *42* (*1* Suppl), 8S–14S.

Golinkoff, R. M., Ma, W., Song, L., & Hirsh-Pasek, K. (2013). Twenty-five years using the intermodal preferential looking paradigm to study language acquisition: What have we learned? *Perspectives on Psychological Science*, *8*, 316–339.

Gosling, S. D., & Mason, W. (2015). Internet research in psychology. *Annual Review of Psychology*, *66*, 877–902.

Gottlieb, G. (1992). *Individual development and evolution*. Oxford: Oxford University Press.

Gredebäck, G., Johnson, S., & von Hofsten, C. (2010). Eye tracking in infancy research. *Developmental Neuropsychology*, *35*, 1–19.

Green, K. B., & Gallagher, P. A. (2014). Mathematics for young children: A review of the literature with implications for children with disabilities. *Başkent University Journal of Education*, *1*, 81–92.

Greenspan, S. I., & Woods, G. W. (2014). Intellectual disability as a disorder of reasoning and judgement: The gradual move away from intelligence quotient-ceilings. *Current Opinion in Psychiatry*, *27*, 110–116.

Grigorenko, E. L. (2009). Dynamic assessment and response to intervention: Two sides of one coin. *Journal of Learning Disabilities*, *42*, 111–132.

Grigorenko, E. L., Klin, A., & Volkmar, F. (2003). Annotation: Hyperlexia: Disability or superability? *Journal of Child Psychology and Psychiatry*, *44*, 1079–1091.

Gross, H., Shaw, D. S., Burwell, R. A., & Nagin, D. S. (2009). Transactional processes in child disruptive behavior and maternal depression: A longitudinal study from early childhood to adolescence. *Development and Psychopathology*, *21*, 139–156.

Guthke, J. (1993). Development in learning potential assessment. In J. H. M. Hamers, K. Sijtsma & A. J. J. M. Ruijssenaars (Eds), *Learning potential assessment* (pp. 43–67). Amsterdam, NL: Swets and Zeitlinger.

Guyon-Harris, K. L., Humphreys, K. L., Fox, N. A., Nelson, C. A., & Zeanah, C. H. (2018). Course of disinhibited social engagement disorder from early childhood to early adolescence. *Journal of the American Academy of Child and Adolescent Psychiatry*, *57*, 329–335.

Halford, G. S. (1989). Reflections on 25 years of Piagetian cognitive psychology. *Human Development*, *32*, 325–357.

Hammack, P. L. (2008). Narrative and the cultural psychology of identity. *Personality and Social Psychology Review*, *12*, 222–247.

Handler, S. M., Fierson, W. M., & The Section on Ophthalmology and Council on Children with Disabilities, American Academy of Ophthalmology, American Association for Pediatric Ophthalmology and Strabismus (2011). Learning disabilities, dyslexia, and vision. *Pediatrics*, *127*, e818–e856.

Hankin, B. L., & Abramson, L. Y. (2001). Development of sex differences in depression: An elaborated cognitive vulnerability–transactional stress theory. *Psychological Bulletin*, *127*, 773–796.

Hankin, B. L., Young, J. F., Gallop, R., & Garber, J. (2018). Cognitive and inter-personal vulnerabilities to adolescent depression: Classification of risk profiles for a personalized prevention approach. *Journal of Abnormal Child Psychology, 46,* 1521–1533 doi.org/10.1007/s10802-018-0401-2.

Harrison, L. J., & McLeod, S. (2010). Risk and protective factors associated with speech and language impairment in a nationally representative sample of 4-to-5-year-old children. *Journal of Speech, Language, and Hearing Research, 53,* 508–529.

Hastings, E. C., Karas, T. L., Winsler, A., Way, E., Madigan, A., & Tyler, S. (2009). Young children's video/computer game use: Relations with school performance and behavior. *Issues in Mental Health Nursing, 30,* 638–649.

Helland, I. B., Smith, L., Saarem, K., Saugstad, O. D., & Drevon, C. A. (2003). Maternal supplementation with very-long-chain n-3 fatty acids during preg-nancy and lactation augments children's IQ at 4 years of age. *Pediatrics, 111,* e39–e44.

Herbart, J. F. (1841). *Umriss pädagogischer Vorlesungen.* Göttingen, Germany: Göt-tingen Druck.

Hinde, R. A. (1992). Human social development: An ethological/relationship perspective. In H. McGurk (Ed.), *Childhood social development: Contemporary perspectives* (pp. 13–29). Hove, UK: Lawrence Erlbaum.

Hinshaw, S. P. (2018). Attention deficit hyperactivity disorder (ADHD): Con-troversy, developmental mechanisms, and multiple levels of analysis. *Annual Review of Clinical Psychology, 14,* 291–316.

Hinshaw, S. P., & Scheffler, R. M. (2014). *The ADHD explosion: Myths, medica-tion, money, and today's push for performance.* Oxford: Oxford University Press.

Hogan, A. E., & Quay, H. C. (2014). Bringing a developmental perspective to early childhood and family interventionists: Where to begin. *Advances in Child Development and Behavior, 46,* 245–279.

Hoogenhout, M., & Malcolm-Smith, S. (2014). Theory of mind in autism spectrum disorder: Does DSM classification predict development? *Research in Autism Spectrum Disorders, 8,* 597–607.

Hoon, A. H., & Tolley, F. (2012). Cerebral palsy. In G. Lotrecchiano, N. Roizen & M. Batshaw (Eds), *Children with disabilities, Seventh edition* (pp. 423–450). Baltimore, MD: Brookes.

Hopkins, B., & Butterworth, G. (1997). Dynamical systems approaches to development of action. In G. Bremner, A. Slater & G. Butterworth (Eds), *Infant development: Recent advances* (pp. 75–100). Hove, UK: Lawrence Erlbaum.

Huber-Okrainec, J., Blaser, S. E., & Dennis, M. (2005). Idiom comprehension deficits in relation to corpus callosum agenesis and hypoplasia in children with spina bifida meningomyelocele. *Brain and Language, 93,* 349–368.

Hughes, C., & Leekam, S. (2004). What are the links between theory of mind and social relations? Review, reflections and new directions for studies of typical and atypical development. *Social Development, 13,* 590–619.

Hughes, J. R. (2009). Update on autism: A review of 1300 reports published in 2008. *Epilepsy and Behavior, 16,* 569–589.

Jeltova, I., Birney, D., Fredine, N., Jarvin, L., Sternberg, R. J., & Grigorenko, E. L. (2007). Dynamic assessment as a process-oriented assessment in educational settings. *Advances in Speech Language Pathology, 9,* 273–285.

Jensen, L. A. (2012). Bridging universal and cultural perspectives: A vision for developmental psychology in a global world. *Child Development Perspectives, 6,* 98–104.

Johansson, A., & Götestam, K. G. (2004). Internet addiction: Characteristics of a questionnaire and prevalence in Norwegian youth (12–18 years). *Scandinavian Journal of Psychology, 45,* 223–229.

John, A., Halliburton, A., & Humphrey, J. (2013). Child–mother and child–father play interaction patterns with preschoolers. *Early Child Development and Care, 183,* 483–497.

Josephs, I. E., & Valsiner, J. (2007). Developmental science meets culture: Cultural developmental psychology in the making. *European Journal of Developmental Science, 1,* 47–64.

Kagan, J. (2008a). In defense of qualitative changes in development. *Child Development, 79,* 1606–1624.

Kagan, J. (2008b). Using the proper vocabulary. *Developmental Psychobiology, 50,* 4–8.

Kagan, J., & Snidman, N. C. (2004). *The long shadow of temperament.* Cambridge, MA: Belknap Press.

Kail, R. V., & Bisanz, J. (1992). The information-processing perspective on cognitive development in childhood and adolescence. In R. J. Sternberg & C. A. Berg (Eds), *Intellectual development* (pp. 229–260). Cambridge: Cambridge University Press.

Kaiser, A. P., & Roberts, M. Y. (2011). Advances in early communication and language intervention. *Journal of Early Intervention, 33,* 298–309.

Kanner, L. (1943). Autistic disturbances of affective contact. *Nervous Child, 12,* 17–50.

Karpov, Y. V. (2005). *The neo-Vygotskian approach to child development.* Cambridge: Cambridge University Press.

Kavale, K. A., Holdnack, J. A., & Mostert, M. P. (2005). Responsiveness to intervention and the identification of specific learning disability: A critique and alternative proposal. *Learning Disability Quarterly, 29,* 113–127.

Keller, H. (2016). Psychological autonomy and hierarchical relatedness as organizers of developmental pathways. *Philosophical Transactions of the Royal Society B: Biological Sciences, 371 (1686),* 1–9.

Kelly-Vance, L., Ryalls, B. O., & Gill-Glover, K. (2002). The use of play assessment to evaluate the cognitive skills of two- and three-year-old children. *School Psychology International, 23,* 169–185.

Kendall, P. C., Peterman, J. S., & Cummings, C. M. (2015). Cognitive-behavioral therapy, behavioral therapy, and related treatments in children. In A. Thapar,

D. S. Pine, F. S. Leckman, S. Scott, M. J. Snowling & E. Taylor (Eds), *Rutter's child and adolescent psychiatry, Sixth edition* (pp. 496–509). Oxford: Wiley.

Kerns, C. M., & Kendall, P. C. (2014). Autism and anxiety: Overlap, similarities, and differences. In T. E. Davis III, S. W. White & T. H. Ollendick (Eds), *Handbook of autism and anxiety* (pp. 75–89). New York, NY: Springer.

Key, E. (1900). *Barnets århundrade: Studie.* Stockholm: Bonniers.

King, D. L., Haagsma, M. C., Delfabbro, P. H., Gradisar, M. S., & Griffiths, M. D. (2013). Toward a consensus definition of pathological video-gaming: A systematic review of psychometric assessment tools. *Clinical Psychology Review, 33,* 331–342.

King, S., Waschbusch, D. A., Pelham Jr, W. E., Frankland, B. W., Andrade, B. F., Jacques, S., & Corkum, P. V. (2009). Social information processing in elementary-school aged children with ADHD: Medication effects and comparisons with typical children. *Journal of Abnormal Child Psychology, 37,* 579–589.

Klein, M. (1948). A contribution to the theory of anxiety and guilt. In *The writings of Melanie Klein,* Volume 1 (pp. 25–42). New York, NY: The Free Press.

Koelch, M., Singer, H., Prestel, A., Burkert, J., Schulze, U., & Fegert, J. M. (2009). ". . . because I am something special" or "I think I will be something like a guinea pig": Information and assent of legal minors in clinical trials – assessment of understanding, appreciation and reasoning. *Child and Adolescent Psychiatry and Mental Health, 3,* 1–13.

Kohlberg, L. (1981). *The philosophy of moral development: Moral stages and the idea of justice.* New York, NY: Harper and Row.

Kohut, H. (1977). *The restoration of the self.* New York, NY: International Universities Press.

Kozulin, A., Gindis, B., Ageyev, V. S., & Miller, S. M. (Eds) (2003). *Vygotsky's educational theory in cultural context.* Cambridge: Cambridge University Press.

Kurmanaviciute, R., & Stadskleiv, K. (2017). Assessment of verbal comprehension and non-verbal reasoning when standard response mode is challenging: A comparison of different response modes and an exploration of their clinical usefulness. *Cogent Psychology, 4,* 1275416.

Kurzban, R., Burton-Chellew, M. N., & West, S. A. (2015). The evolution of altruism in humans. *Annual Review of Psychology, 66,* 575–599.

Kuss, D. J., van Rooij, A., Shorter, G. W., Griffiths, M. D., & van de Mheen, D. (2013). Internet addiction in adolescents: Prevalence and risk factors. *Computers in Human Behavior, 29,* 1987–1996.

Lambek, R., Sonuga-Barke, E., Psychogiou, L., Thompson, M., Tannock, R., Daley, D., Damm, D., & Thomson, P. H. (2017). The Parental Emotional Response to Children Index. A questionnaire measure of parents' reactions to ADHD. *Journal of Attention Disorders, 21,* 494–507.

Laraway, S., Snycerski, S., Michael, J., & Poling, A. (2003). Motivating operations and terms to describe them: Some further refinements. *Journal of Applied Behavior Analysis, 3,* 407–414.

Largo, R. H., Kundu, S., & Thun-Hohenstein, L. (1993). Early motor development in term and preterm children. In A. F. Kalverboer, B. Hopkins & R. Geuze (Eds), *Motor development in early and later childhood: Longitudinal approaches* (pp. 247–265). Cambridge: Cambridge University Press.

Lave, J., & Wenger, E. (1991). *Situated learning*. Cambridge: Cambridge University Press.

Leaper, C., & Smith, T. E. (2004). A meta-analytic review of gender variations in children's language use: Talkativeness, affiliative speech, and assertive speech. *Developmental Psychology, 40*, 993–1027.

Leekam, S. (2016). Social cognitive impairment and autism: What are we trying to explain? *Philosophical Transactions of the Royal Society B: Biological Sciences, 371* (1686), 20150082.

Leibenluft, E., & Dickstein, D. P. (2015). Bipolar disorder in childhood. In A. Thapar, D. S. Pine, F. S. Leckman, S. Scott, M. J. Snowling & E. Taylor (Eds), *Rutter's child and adolescent psychiatry, Sixth edition* (pp. 866–873). Oxford: Wiley.

Lerner, R. M. (2002). *Concepts and theories of human development, Third edition.* Mahwah, NJ: Erlbaum.

Lerner, R. M., & Castellino, D. R. (2002). Contemporary developmental theory and adolescence: Developmental systems and applied developmental science. *Journal of Adolescent Health, 31*, 122–135.

Lerner, R. M., Schwartz, S. J., & Phelps, E. (2009). Problematics of time and timing in the longitudinal study of human development: Theoretical and methodological issues. *Human Development, 52*, 44–68.

Lewin, K. (1931). Environmental forces in child behavior and development. In C. Murchison (Ed.), *A handbook of child development, Second edition* (pp. 590–625). Worcester, MA: Clark University Press.

Lewis, M., & Rudolph, K. (Eds) (2014). *Handbook of developmental psychopathology, Third edition.* New York, NY: Springer.

Lickliter, R., & Honeycutt, H. (2015). Biology, development, and human systems. In R. M. Lerner, W. F. Overton & P. C. M. Molenaar (Eds), *Handbook of child psychology and developmental science, Seventh edition. Volume 1: Theory and method* (pp. 162–207). New York, NY: Wiley.

Lidz, C. S. (1997). Dynamic assessment approaches. In D. P. Flanagan, J. L. Genshaft & P. L. Harrison (Eds), *Contemporary intellectual assessment. Theories, tests, and issues* (pp. 281–296). London: Guilford Press.

Lidz, C. S., & Peña, E. D. (2009). Response to intervention and dynamic assessment: Do we just appear to be speaking the same language? *Seminars in Speech and Language, 30*, 121–133.

Lieberman, A. F., Compton, N. C., Van Horn, P., & Ghosh Ippen, C. (2003). *Losing a caregiver to death in the early years: Guidelines for the treatment of traumatic bereavement in infancy and early childhood.* Washington, DC: Zero to Three.

Little, A. H., Lipsitt, L. P., & Rovee-Collier, C. (1984). Classical conditioning and retention of the infant's eyelid response: Effects of age and interstimulus interval. *Journal of Experimental Child Psychology, 37*, 512–524.

Lord, C., Bishop, S., & Anderson, D. (2015, June). Developmental trajectories as autism phenotypes. *American Journal of Medical Genetics Part C: Seminars in Medical Genetics, 169*, 198–208.

Lorenz, K. (1935). Der Kumpan in der Umvelt des Vogels. *Journal für Ornithologie, 83*, 137–213 & 289–413.

Lourenço, O. M. (2016). Developmental stages, Piagetian stages in particular: A critical review. *New Ideas in Psychology, 40*, 123–137.

Lovaas, O. I. (1993). The development of a treatment-research project for developmentally disabled and autistic children. *Journal of Applied Behavior Analysis, 26*, 617–630.

Luborsky, L., & Barrett, M. S. (2006). The history and empirical status of key psychoanalytic concepts. *Annual Review of Clinical Psychology, 2*, 1–19.

Lund, T. (2005). The qualitative–quantitative distinction: Some comments. *Scandinavian Journal of Educational Research, 49*, 115–132.

Luria, A. R. (1961). *The role of speech in the regulation of normal and abnormal behavior*. Oxford: Pergamon Press.

Luthar, S. S., Lyman, E. L., & Crossman, E. J. (2014). Resilience and positive psychology. In M. Lewis & K. Rudolph (Eds), *Handbook of developmental psychopathology* (pp. 125–140). New York, NY: Springer.

Macintyre, C. (2000). *Dyspraxia in the early years. Identifying and supporting children with movement difficulties*. London: David Fulton Publishers.

Macintyre, C. (2001). *Dyspraxia 5–11: A practical guide*. London: David Fulton Publishers.

Macy, M. (2012). The evidence behind developmental screening instruments. *Infants and Young Children, 25*, 19–61.

Madge, N., & Fassam, M. (1982). *Ask the children. Experiences of physical disability in the school years*. London: Batsford.

Magnus, P., Birke, C., Vejrup, K., Haugan, A., Alsaker, E., Daltveit, A. K., Handal, M., Haugen, M., Høiseth, G., Knudsen, G. P., et al. (2016). Cohort profile update: The Norwegian mother and child cohort study (MoBa). *International Journal of Epidemiology, 45*, 382–388.

Mahler, M. S., Pine, F., & Bergman, A. (1975). *The psychological birth of the human infant symbiosis and individuation*. New York, NY: Basic Books.

Marchand, H. (2012). Contributions of Piagetian and post-Piagetian theories to education. *Educational Research Review, 7*, 165–176.

Marfo, K. (2011). Envisioning an African child development field. *Child Development Perspectives, 5*, 140–147.

Marschark, M., Schick, B., & Spencer, P. E. (2006). Understanding sign language development of deaf children. In B. Schick, M. Marschark & P. E. Spencer (Eds), *Advances in the sign language development of deaf children* (pp. 3–19). New York, NY: Oxford University Press.

Marschark, M., Spencer, P. E., Adams, J., & Sapere, P. (2011). Evidence-based practice in educating deaf and hard-of-hearing children: Teaching to their cognitive strengths and needs. *European Journal of Special Needs Education, 26,* 3–16.

Martí, E., & Rodríguez, C. (Eds) (2012). *After Piaget.* New Brunswick, NJ: Transaction Publishers.

Massaro, D. W., & Cowan, N. (1993). Information processing models: Microscopes of the mind. *Annual Review of Psychology, 44,* 383–425.

Masten, A. S., & Cicchetti, D. (2010). Developmental cascades. *Development and Psychopathology, 22,* 491–495.

Matson, J. L., & Kozlowski, A. M. (2011). The increasing prevalence of autism spectrum disorders. *Research in Autism Spectrum Disorders, 5,* 418–425.

McGoron, L., Gleason, M. M., Smyke, A. T., Drury, S. S., Nelson, C. A., III, Gregas, M. C., Fox, N. A., & Zeanah, C. H. (2012). Recovering from early deprivation: Attachment mediates effects of caregiving on psychopathology. *Journal of the American Academy of Child and Adolescent Psychiatry, 51,* 683–693.

Mendez, L. M. R. (2017). *Cognitive behavioral therapy in schools: A tiered approach to youth mental health services.* New York, NY: Routledge.

Messias, E., Castro, J., Saini, A., Usman, M., & Peeples, D. (2011). Sadness, suicide, and their association with video game and Internet overuse among teens: Results from the Youth Risk Behavior Survey 2007 and 2009. *Suicide and Life-Threatening Behavior, 41,* 307–315.

Miao, X., & Wang, W. (2003). A century of Chinese developmental psychology. *International Journal of Psychology, 38,* 258–273.

Miller, C. A. (2001). False belief understanding in children with specific language impairment. *Journal of Communication Disorders, 34,* 73–86.

Miller, C. A. (2011). Auditory processing theories of language disorders: Past, present, and future. *Language, Speech, and Hearing Services in Schools, 42,* 309–319.

Miller, M. R., Müller, U., Giesbrecht, G. F., Carpendale, J. I., & Kerns, K. A. (2013). The contribution of executive function and social understanding to preschoolers' letter and math skills. *Cognitive Development, 28,* 331–349.

Miller, R. S. (2007). Is embarrassment a blessing or a curse? In J. L. Tracy, R. W. Robins & J. P. Tangney (Eds), *The self-conscious emotions: Theory and research* (pp. 245–262). New York, NY: Oxford University Press.

Millum, J., & Emanuel, E. J. (2007). The ethics of international research with abandoned children. *Science, 318,* 1874–1875.

Mitchell, L. E., Adzick, N. S., Melchionne, J., Pasquariello, P. S., Sutton, L. N., & Whitehead, A. S. (2004). Spina bifida. *Lancet, 364,* 1885–1895.

Mitchell, R. E., & Karchmer, M. A. (2006). Demographics of deaf education: More students in more places. *American Annals of the Deaf, 151,* 95–104.

Mitchell, S. A. (1988). *Relational concepts in psychoanalysis.* Cambridge, MA: Harvard University Press.

Mole, S. E., Williams, R. E., & Goebbel, H. H. (2011). *The neuronal ceroid lipofus-cinoses (Batten disease), Second edition.* Oxford: Oxford University Press.

Morgan, G., Herman, R., & Woll, B. (2007). Language impairments in sign language: Breakthroughs and puzzles. *International Journal of Language and Communication Disorders, 42,* 97–105.

Morra, S., Gobbo, C., Marini, Z., & Sheese, R. (2008). *Cognitive development: Neo-Piagetian perspectives.* New York, NY: Lawrence Erlbaum.

Morss, J. R. (1996). *Growing critical: Alternatives to developmental psychology.* London: Routledge.

Moultrie, R. R., Kish-Doto, J., Peay, H., & Lewis, M. A. (2016). A review on spinal muscular atrophy: Awareness, knowledge, and attitudes. *Journal of Genetic Counseling, 25,* 892–900.

Nation, K., & Norbury, C. F. (2005). Why reading comprehension fails: Insights from developmental disorders. *Topics in Language Disorders, 25,* 21–32.

Nelson, K. (2007). *Young minds in social worlds: Experience, meaning and memory.* Cambridge, MA: Harvard University Press.

Nelson, K. (2015). Quantitative and qualitative research in psychological science. *Biological Theory, 10,* 263–272.

Nielsen, M., & Haun, D. (2016). Why developmental psychology is incomplete without comparative and cross-cultural perspectives. *Philosophical Transactions of the Royal Society B: Biological Sciences, 371 (1686),* 1–7.

Nomura, K., Okada, K., Noujima, Y., Kojima, S., Mori, Y., Amano, M., Ogura, M., Hatagaki, C., Shibata, Y., & Fukumoto, R. (2014). A clinical study of attention deficit/hyperactivity disorder in preschool children – Prevalence and differential diagnoses. *Brain and Development, 36,* 778–785.

Nsamenang, B. A., & Lo-Oh, J. L. (2010). Afrique Noire. In M. H. Bornstein (Ed.), *Handbook of cultural developmental science* (pp. 383–408). New York, NY: Psychology Press.

O'Neill, Y. V. (1980). *Speech and speech disorders in Western thought before 1600.* London: Greenwood Press.

Odgers, C. L., Moffitt, T. E., Broadbent, J. M., Dickson, N. P., Hancox, R., Harrington, H., Poulton, R., Sears, M. R., Thompson, W. M., & Caspi, A. (2008). Female and male antisocial trajectories: From childhood origins to adult outcomes. *Development and Psychopathology, 20,* 673–716.

Onishi, K. H., & Baillargeon, R. (2005). Do 15-month-old infants understand false beliefs? *Science, 308,* 255–258.

Ortigo, K. M., Bradley, B., & Westen, D. (2010). An empirically based prototype diagnostic system for DSM–V and ICD–11. In T. Millon, R. Krueger & E. Simonsen (Eds), *Contemporary directions in psychopathology: Scientific foundations of the DSM–V and ICD–11* (pp. 374–390). New York, NY: Guilford Press.

Overton, W. F. (2015). Processes, relations, and relational-developmental-systems. In R. M. Lerner, W. F. Overton & P. C. M. Molenaar (Eds), *Handbook of child psychology and developmental science, Seventh edition, Volume 1: Theory and method* (pp. 9–62). Hoboken, NJ: Wiley.

Palacios, J., & Brodzinsky, D. (2010). Adoption research: Trends, topics, outcomes. *International Journal of Behavioral Development, 34,* 270–284.

Parker, R. I., & Hagan-Burke, S. (2007). Single case research results as clinical outcomes. *The Journal of School Psychology, 45,* 637–653.

Pascual-Leone, J. (1970). A mathematical model for the transition rule in Piaget's developmental stages. *Acta Psychologica, 32,* 301–345.

Pennington, B. F., McGrath, L. M., Rosenberg, J., Barnard, H., Smith, S. D., Willcutt, E. G., Friend, A., DeFires, J. C., & Olson, R. K. (2009). Gene-environment interactions in reading disability and attention deficit/ hyperactivity disorder. *Developmental Psychology, 45,* 77–89.

Pérez-Pereira, M., & Conti-Ramsden, G. (1999). *Language development and social interaction in blind children.* Hove, UK: Psychology Press.

Peterson, R. L., & Pennington, B. F. (2015). Developmental dyslexia. *Annual Review of Clinical Psychology, 11,* 283–307.

Pfeiffer, J. P., & Pinquart, M. (2014). Bullying in German boarding schools: A pilot study. *School Psychology International, 35,* 580–591.

Piaget, J. (1950). *The psychology of the child.* London: Routledge and Kegan Paul.

Piaget, J. (1952). *The origin of intelligence in the child.* London: Routledge and Kegan Paul.

Piaget, J. (1954). *The construction of reality in the child.* New York, NY: Routledge and Kegan Paul.

Piaget, J. (1959). *The language and thought of the child, Third edition.* London: Routledge.

Piaget, J. (1970). *The child's conception of movement and speed.* London: Routledge and Kegan Paul.

Piaget, J., Henriques, G., & Ascher, E. (Eds). (1992). *Morphisms and categories: Comparing and transforming*. London: Lawrence Erlbaum.

Pine, D. S., & Klein, R. G. (2015). Anxiety disorders. In A. Thapar, D. S. Pine, F. S. Leckman, S. Scott, M. J. Snowling & E. Taylor (Eds), *Rutter's child and adolescent psychiatry,* Sixth edition (pp. 822–840). Oxford: Wiley.

Pinhas, L., Morris, A., Crosby, R. D., & Katzman, D. K. (2011). Incidence and age-specific presentation of restrictive eating disorders in children: A Canadian Paediatric Surveillance Program study. *Archives of Pediatrics and Adolescent Medicine, 165,* 895–899.

Pinker, S. (1994). *The language instinct.* London: Allen Lane.

Pinker, S. (1997). *How the mind works.* New York, NY: Norton.

Pluess, M., & Belsky, J. (2013). Vantage sensitivity: Individual differences in response to positive experiences. *Psychological Bulletin, 139,* 901–916.

Popper, K. R. (1959). *The logic of scientific discovery.* London: Hutchinson.

Preyer, W. (1882/1988). *The mind of the child.* New York, NY: Appleton.

Racz, S. J., Putnick, D. L., Suwalsky, J. T., Hendricks, C., & Bornstein, M. H. (2017). Cognitive abilities, social adaptation, and externalizing behavior problems in childhood and adolescence: Specific cascade effects across development. *Journal of Youth and Adolescence, 46*, 1688–1701.

Raghubar, K. P., Barnes, M. A., & Hecht, S. A. (2010). Working memory and mathematics: A review of developmental, individual difference, and cognitive approaches. *Learning and Individual Differences, 20*, 110–122.

Rapin, I., Dunn, M. A., Allen, D. A., Stevens, M. C., & Fein, D. (2009). Subtypes of language disorders in school-age children with autism. *Developmental Neuropsychology, 34*, 66–84.

Reese, H. W. (1999). Strategies for replication research exemplified by replications of the Istomina study. *Developmental Review, 19*, 1–30.

Reesman, J. H., Day, L. A., Szymanski, C. A., Hughes-Wheatland, R., Witkin, G. A., Kalback, S. R., & Brice, P. J. (2014). Review of intellectual assessment measures for children who are deaf or hard of hearing. *Rehabilitation Psychology, 59*, 99–106.

Rescorla, L. A., Bochicchio, L., Achenbach, T. M., Ivanova, M. Y., Almqvist, F., Begovac, I., Bilenberg, N., Bird, H., Dobrean, A., Erol, N., et al. (2014). Parent–teacher agreement on children's problems in 21 societies. *Journal of Clinical Child and Adolescent Psychology, 43*, 627–642.

Reznick, J. S. (2013). Research design and methods: Toward a cumulative developmental science. In P. D. Zelazo (Ed.), *The Oxford handbook of developmental psychology, Volume 1: Body and mind* (pp. 35–61). Oxford: Oxford University Press.

Richards, J. E. (2001). Cortical indices of saccade planning in infants. *Infancy, 2*, 123–133.

Ricketts, J. (2011). Research review: Reading comprehension in developmental disorders of language and communication. *Journal of Child Psychology and Psychiatry, 52*, 1111–1123.

Rizzolatti, G. (2005). The mirror neuron system and its function in humans. *Anatomy and Embryology, 210*, 419–421.

Roessner, V., Ehrlich, S., & Vetter, N. C. (2016). Child and adolescent psychiatry in ICD-11: An opportunity to overcome mistakes made in DSM-5? *European Child and Adolescent Psychiatry, 9*, 935–938.

Roisman, G. I., Newman, D. A., Fraley, R. C., Haltigan, J. D., Groh, A. M., & Haydon, K. C. (2012). Distinguishing differential susceptibility from diathesis–stress: Recommendations for evaluating interaction effects. *Development and Psychopathology, 24*, 389–409.

Roopnarine, J. L., & Davidson, K. L. (2015). Parent-child play across cultures: Advancing play research. *American Journal of Play, 7*, 228–252.

Rosenbaum, P., Paneth, N., Leviton, A., Goldstein, M., Bax, M., Damiano, D., Dan, B., & Jacobsson, B. (2007). A report: The definition and classification of cerebral palsy April 2006. *Developmental Medicine and Child Neurology, 49* (Supplement *109*), 8–14.

Rothenberger, A., & Banaschewski, T. (2004). Informing the ADHD debate. *Scientific American Mind, 14 (5)*, 50–55.

Rothenberger, A., & Banaschewski, T. (2007). Informing the ADHD debate. *Scientific American, 17*, 36–41.

Rousseau, J. (1763). *Emile, or, concerning education.* London: Heath and Company.

Rovee-Collier, C., & Barr, R. (2001). Infant learning and memory. In J. G. Bremner & A. Fogel (Eds), *Blackwell handbook of infant development* (pp. 139–168). Oxford: Blackwell.

Rovee-Collier, C., & Cuevas, K. (2009a). The development of infant memory. In M. L. Courage & N. Cowan (Eds), *The development of memory in infancy and childhood*, Second edition (pp. 11–41). New York, NY: Psychology Press.

Ruban, L. M., & Reis, S. M. (2005). Identification and assessment of gifted students with learning disabilities. *Theory into Practice, 44*, 115–124.

Rubin, K. H., & Coplan, R. J. (Eds) (2010). *The development of shyness and social withdrawal.* New York, NY: Guilford Press.

Rutter, M. (2005). Environmentally mediated risks for psychopathology: Research strategies and findings. *Journal of American Academy of Child and Adolescent Psychiatry, 44*, 3–18.

Rutter, M. (2013). Annual research review: Resilience—clinical implications. *Journal of Child Psychology and Psychiatry, 54*, 474–487.

Rutter, M. (2014). Nature-nurture integration. In M. Lewis & K. Rudolph (Eds), *Handbook of developmental psychopathology*, Third edition (pp. 45–65). New York, NY: Springer.

Rutter, M., Kim-Cohen, J., & Maughan, B. (2006). Continuities and discontinuities in psychopathology between childhood and adult life. *Journal of Child Psychology and Psychiatry, 47*, 276–295.

Rutter, M., & Pine, D. S. (2015). Diagnosis, diagnostic formulation and classification. In A. Thapar, D. S. Fine, J. F. Leckman, S. Scott, M. J. Snowling & E. Taylor (Eds), *Rutter's child and adolescent psychiatry* (pp. 17–30). Chichester, UK: Wiley.

Rutter, M., & Sroufe, L. A. (2000). Developmental psychopathology: Concepts and challenges. *Developmental Psychopathology, 12*, 265–296.

Sameroff, A. J. (Ed.) (2009). *The transactional model of development: How children and contexts shape each other.* Washington, DC: American Psychological Association.

Sameroff, A. J. (2010). A unified theory of development: A dialectic integration of nature and nurture. *Child Development, 81*, 6–22.

Sameroff, A. J. (2014). A dialectic integration of development for the study of psychopathology. In M. Lewis & K. Rudolph (Eds), *Handbook of developmental psychopathology* (pp. 25–44). Boston, MA: Springer.

Sanders, M. R. (1996). New directions in behavioral family intervention with children. In T. H. Ollendick & R. J. Prinz (Eds), *Advances in clinical child psychology* (pp. 283–330). Boston, MA: Springer.

Saraswathi, T. S., & Dutta, R. (2010). India. In M. H. Bornstein (Ed.), *Handbook of cultural developmental science* (pp. 465–483). London: Psychology Press.

Sattler, J. M. (2002). *Assessment of children: Behavioral and clinical applications, Fourth edition*. San Diego, CA: J. M. Sattler Publications.

Scarr, S. (1992). Developmental theories for the 1990s: Development and individual differences. *Child Development, 63,* 1–19.

Schaffer, H. R. (1989). Language development in context. In S. von Tetzchner, L. S. Siegel & L. Smith (Eds), *The social and cognitive aspects of normal and atypical language development* (pp. 1–22). New York, NY: Springer.

Schlesinger, M., & McMurray, B. (2012). The past, present, and future of computational models of cognitive development. *Cognitive Development, 27,* 326–348.

Schlinger, H. D. (1995). *A behavior analytic view of child development*. New York, NY: Plenum Press.

Schoenberg, M. R., & Scott, J. G. (2011). Cognitive decline in childhood or young adulthood. In M. R. Schoenberg & J. G. Scott (Eds), *The little black book of neuropsychology: A syndrome-based approach* (pp. 839–861). New York, NY: Springer.

Schöner, G., & Dineva, E. (2007). Dynamic instabilities as mechanisms for emergence. *Developmental Science, 10,* 69–74.

Scollon, R. T. (1976). *Conversations with a one year old*. Honolulu: University of Hawaii Press.

Scott, I. A., & Attia, J. (2017). Cautionary tales in the interpretation of observational studies of effects of clinical interventions. *Internal Medicine Journal, 47,* 144–157.

Scott, S. (2015). Oppositional and conduct disorders. In A. Thapar, D. S. Fine, J. F. Leckman, S. Scott, M. J. Snowling & E. Taylor (Eds), *Rutter's child and adolescent psychiatry* (pp. 913–930). Chichester, UK: Wiley.

Seifer, R., Sameroff, A. J., Barrett, L. C., & Krafchuk, E. (1994). Infant temperament measured by multiple observations and mother report. *Child Development, 65,* 1478–1490.

Seim, S. (1997). Tenåringen blir pensjonist. *NOVA Rapport 23.*

Selb, M., Kohler, F., Nicol, M. M. R., Riberto, M., Stucki, G., Kennedy, C., & Üstün, B. (2015). ICD-11: A comprehensive picture of health, an update on the ICD–ICF joint use initiative. *Journal of Rehabilitation Medicine, 47,* 2–8.

Seligman, M., & Darling, R. B. (2007). *Ordinary families, special children: A systems approach to childhood disability*, Third edition. London: Guilford Press.

Selin, H. (2014). *Parenting across cultures*. Dordrecht, The Netherlands: Springer.

Shaw, P., Stringaris, A., Nigg, J., & Leibenluft, E. (2014). Emotion dysregulation in attention deficit hyperactivity disorder. *American Journal of Psychiatry, 171,* 276–293.

Shaywitz, S. E., Morris, R., & Shaywitz, B. A. (2008). The education of dyslexic children from childhood to young adulthood. *Annual Review of Psychology, 59,* 451–475.

Siegler, R. S. (2006). Microgenetic analyses of learning. In W. Damon, R. M. Lerner, D. Kuhn & R. S. Siegler (Eds), *Handbook of child psychology, Sixth edition, Volume 2: Cognition, perception, and language* (pp. 464–510). Hoboken, NJ: Wiley.

Simms, M. D. (2007). Language disorders in children: Classification and clinical syndromes. *Pediatric Clinics of North America, 54*, 437–467.

Simon, H. A. (1962). An information processing theory of intellectual development. *Monographs of the Society for Research in Child Development*, 150–161.

Skinner, B. F. (1938). *The behavior of organisms*. New York, NY: Appleton-Century-Crofts.

Skinner, B. F. (1971). *Beyond freedom and dignity*. New York, NY: Knopf.

Skinner, B. F. (1977). Why I am not a cognitive psychologist. *Behaviorism, 5*, 1–10.

Skinner, B. F. (1981). Selection by consequences. *Science, 213 (4507)*, 501–504.

Skinner, B. F. (1984). The phylogeny and ontogeny of behavior. *Behavioral and Brain Sciences, 7*, 669–677.

Skogli, E. W., Teicher, M. H., Andersen, P. N., Hovik, K. T., & Øie, M. (2013). ADHD in girls and boys – gender differences in co-existing symptoms and executive function measures. *BMC Psychiatry, 13*, 298.

Skretting, A., Lund, K. E., & Bye, E. K. (2014). *Rusmidler i Norge* (Drugs in Norway). Oslo: Statens institutt for rusmidler.

Smith, D. W., & Amato, S. (2012). Synthesis of available accommodations for students with visual impairments on standardized assessments. *Journal of Visual Impairment and Blindness, 106*, 299–304.

Smith, L. B., & Thelen, E. (2003). Development as a dynamic system. *Trends in Cognitive Sciences, 7*, 343–348.

Sommer, D. (2012). *A childhood psychology: Young children in changing times*. New York, NY: Palgrave Macmillan.

Sonuga-Barke, E. J. S., & Taylor, E. (2015). ADHD and hypergenetic disorder. In A. Thapar, D. S. Fine, J. F. Leckman, S. Scott, M. J. Snowling & E. Taylor (Eds), *Rutter's child and adolescent psychiatry* (pp. 738–756). Chichester, UK: Wiley.

Sparrow, S. S., Ciccetti, D. V., & Balla, D. A. (2005). *Vineland Adaptive Behavior Scales, Second edition*. Circle Pines, MN: American Guidance Service.

Spelke, E. S., & Kinzler, K. D. (2007). Core knowledge. *Developmental Science, 10*, 89–96.

Spence, I., & Feng, J. (2010). Video games and spatial cognition. *Review of General Psychology, 14*, 92–104.

Spencer, J. P., & Perone, S. (2008). Defending qualitative change: The view from dynamical systems theory. *Child Development, 79*, 1639–1647.

Sroufe, L. A. (1997). Psychopathology as an outcome of development. *Development and Psychopathology, 9*, 251–268.

Sroufe, L. A. (2007). The place of development in developmental psychopathology. In A. S. Masten (Ed.), *Multilevel dynamics in developmental psychopathology: Pathways to the future* (pp. 285–299). New York, NY: Lawrence Erlbaum.

Sroufe, L. A., Coffino, B., & Carlson, E. A. (2010). Conceptualizing the role of early experience: Lessons from the Minnesota longitudinal study. *Developmental Review, 30*, 36–51.

Stadskleiv, K., Jahnsen, R., Andersen, G. L., & von Tetzchner, S. (2017). Neuropsychological profiles of children with cerebral palsy. *Developmental Neurorehabilitation, 28*, 108–120.

Steinhausen, H. C., Wachter, M., Laimböck, K., & Metzke, C. W. (2006). A long-term outcome study of selective mutism in childhood. *Journal of Child Psychology and Psychiatry, 47*, 751–756.

Steinman, K. J., Mostofsky, S. H., & Denckla, M. B. (2010). Toward a narrower, more pragmatic view of developmental dyspraxia. *Journal of Child Neurology, 25*, 71–81.

Stenberg, N., Bresnahan, M., Gunnes, N., Hirtz, D., Hornig, M., Lie, K. K., Lipkin, W. I., Lord, C., Magnus, P., Reichborn-Kjennerud, T., et al. (2014). Identifying children with autism spectrum disorder at 18 months in a general population sample. *Paediatric and Perinatal Epidemiology, 28*, 255–262.

Stern, D. N. (1998). *The interpersonal world of the infant: A view from psychoanalysis and developmental psychology*. New York, NY: Karnac Books.

Stern, W. (1912). *The psychological methods of testing intelligence*. Baltimore, MD: Warwick and York.

Sternberg, R. J. (2014). The development of adaptive competence: Why cultural psychology is necessary and not just nice. *Developmental Review, 34*, 208–224.

Stetsenko, A., & Arievitch, I. M. (2004). The self in cultural-historical activity theory: Reclaiming the unity of social and individual dimensions of human development. *Theory and Psychology, 14*, 475–503.

Stoiber, K. C., Purdy, S., & Klingbeil, D. A. (2016). Evidence-based practices. In N. N. Singh (Ed.), *Handbook of evidence-based practices in intellectual and developmental disabilities* (pp. 41–68). Cham, Switzerland: Springer.

Stroebe, W. (2016). Are most published social psychological findings false? *Journal of Experimental Social Psychology, 66*, 134–144.

Stroebe, W., Postmes, T., & Spears, R. (2012). Scientific misconduct and the myth of self-correction in science. *Perspectives on Psychological Science, 7*, 670–688.

Strømme, P., & Valvatne, K. (1998). Mental retardation in Norway: Prevalence and subclassification in a cohort of 30 037 children born between 1980 and 1985. *Acta Pædiatrica, 87*, 291–296.

Supkoff, L. M., Puig, J., & Sroufe, L. A. (2012). Situating resilience in developmental context. In M. Ungar (Ed.), *The social ecology of resilience* (pp. 127–142). New York, NY: Springer.

Tafreshi, D., Thompson, J. J., & Racine, T. P. (2014). An analysis of the conceptual foundations of the infant preferential looking paradigm. *Human Development, 57*, 222–240.

Tappan, M. B. (2006). Mediated moralities: Sociocultural approaches to moral development. In M. Killen & J. G. Smetana (Eds), *Handbook of moral development* (pp. 351–374). Mahwah, NJ: Erlbaum.

Tardif, T., & Miao, X. (2000). Developmental psychology in China. *International Journal of Behavioral Development, 24,* 68–72.

Thapar, A., & Rutter, M. (2015). Neurodevelopmental disorders. In A. Thapar, D. Pine, J. Leckman, S. Scott, M. Snowling & E. Taylor (Eds), *Rutter's child and adolescent psychiatry, Sixth edition* (pp. 31–40). London: Wiley.

Thomas, R. M. (2005). *Comparing theories of child development, Sixth edition.* Belmont, CA: Wadsworth.

Tidmarsh, L. (1997). Mood disorder: Prolonged bereavement/grief reaction. In A. Lieberman, S. Wieder & E. Fenichel (Eds), *DC: 0-3 Case Book* (pp. 69–79). Washington, DC: Zero to Three.

Tiedemann, T. (1787). Beobachtungen über die Entwicklung der Seelesfähigkeiten bei Kindern. *Hessische Beiträge zur Gelehrsamkeit und Kunst, 2 (6–7).*

Tisdale, S., & Pellizzoni, L. (2015). Disease mechanisms and therapeutic approaches in spinal muscular atrophy. *Journal of Neuroscience, 35,* 8691–8700.

Tolan, P. H., & Deutsch, N. L. (2015). Mixed methods in developmental science. In R. M. Lerner, I. W. Overton & P. C. M. Molenaar (Eds), *Handbook of child psychology and developmental science, Seventh edition, Volume 1: Theoretical models of human development* (pp. 713–757). Hoboken, NJ: Wiley.

Tomasello, M. (1992). *First verbs.* Cambridge: Cambridge University Press.

Tone, E. B., & Tully, E. C. (2014). Empathy as a "risky strength": A multilevel examination of empathy and risk for internalizing disorders. *Development and Psychopathology, 26 (4pt2),* 1547–1565.

Tosto, M. G., Petrill, S. A., Halberda, J., Trzaskowski, M., Tikhomirova, T. N., Bogdanova, O. Y., Ly, R., Wilmer, J. B., Naiman, D. Q., Germine, L., et al. (2014). Why do we differ in number sense? Evidence from a genetically sensitive investigation. *Intelligence, 43,* 35–46.

Turner, L. M., & Stone, W. L. (2007). Variability in outcome for children with an ASD diagnosis at age 2. *Journal of Child Psychology and Psychiatry, 48,* 793–802.

Tzuriel, D. (2005). Dynamic assessment of learning potential: A new paradigm. *Transylvanian Journal of Psychology, 1,* 7–16.

Undheim, A. M., & Drugli, M. B. (2012). Age for enrolling in full-time childcare: A qualitative study of parent and caregiver perspectives. *Early Child Development and Care, 182,* 1673–1682.

Valsiner, J. (1987). *Culture and the development of children's action.* New York, NY: Wiley.

Valsiner, J. (2012). *A guided science: History of psychology in the mirror of its making.* New Brunswick, NJ: Transaction Publishers.

van den Eijnden, R. J. J. M., Vermulst, A. A., van Rooij, A., Scholte, R., & van de Mheen, D. (2011). Online and real life victimisation and adolescents' psychosocial problems: What is the cause and what is the consequence? *Psychology and Health, 26,* 204–205.

van der Steen, S., Steenbeek, H., Wielinski, J., & van Geert, P. (2012). A comparison between young students with and without special needs on their understanding of scientific concepts. *Education Research International, 2012* (*260403*), 1–12.

van Geert, P., & Steenbeek, H. (2005). The dynamics of scaffolding. *New Ideas in Psychology, 23,* 115–128.

van Nieuwenhuijzen, M., & Vriens, A. (2012). (Social) Cognitive skills and social information processing in children with mild to borderline intellectual disabilities. *Research in Developmental Disabilities, 33,* 426–434.

Vassilieva, J. (2010). Russian psychology at the turn of the 21st century and post-Soviet reforms in the humanities disciplines. *History of Psychology, 13,* 138–159.

Volkmar, F., Siegel, M., Woodbury-Smith, M., King, B., & McCracken, J. (2014). Practice parameter for the assessment and treatment of children and adolescents with autism spectrum disorder. *Journal of the American Academy of Child and Adolescent Psychiatry, 53,* 237–257.

von Eye, A., Bergman, L. R., & Hsieh, C.-A. (2015). Person-oriented methodological approaches. In R. M. Lerner, W. F. Overton & P. C. M. Molenaar (Eds), *Handbook of child psychology and developmental science, Seventh edition, Volume 1: Theory and method* (pp. 789–841). New York, NY: Wiley.

von Tetzchner, S. (1998). *Noonan syndrome. Characteristics, development, and intervention.* Oslo, Norway: Centre for Rare Disorders, The National Hospital.

von Tetzchner, S., Fosse, P., & Elmerskog, B. (2013). Juvenile neuronal ceroid lipofuscinosis and education. *Biochimica et Biophysica Acta (BBA)-Molecular Basis of Disease, 1832,* 1894–1905.

Vygotsky, L. S. (1962). *Thought and language.* Cambridge, MA: MIT Press.

Vygotsky, L. S. (1978). *Mind in society: The development of higher mental processes.* Cambridge, MA: Harvard University Press.

Wachs, T. D. (2003). Expanding our view of context: The bio-ecological environment and development. In R. Kail, (Ed.). *Advances in child development and behavior,* Vol *31* (pp. 365–411). San Diego, CA: Academic Press.

Wallace, P. (2014). Internet addiction disorder and youth. *EMBO Reports, 15,* 12–16.

Warren, S. F., Brady, N., Sterling, A., Fleming, K., & Marquis, J. (2010). Maternal responsivity predicts language development in young children with Fragile X syndrome. *American Journal on Intellectual and Developmental Disabilities, 115,* 54–57.

Webster-Stratton, C. (2006). *The Incredible Years: A trouble-shooting guide for parents of children aged 3–8.* Seattle, WA: Incredible Years Press.

Weems, C. F., & Varela, R. E. (2011). Generalized anxiety disorder. In D. McKay & E. Storch (Eds), *Handbook of child and adolescent anxiety disorders* (pp. 261–274). New York, NY: Springer.

Weindrich, D., Steinmetz, C. J., Laucht, M., Esser, G., & Schmidt, M. (2000). Epidemiology and prognosis of specific disorders of language and scholastic skills. *European Child and Adolescent Psychiatry, 9,* 186–194.

Wertsch, J. V. (1991). *Voices of the mind: A sociocultural approach to mediated action.* London: Harvester Wheatsheaf.

Westen, D. (1998). The scientific legacy of Sigmund Freud: Toward a psychodynamically informed psychological science. *Psychological Bulletin, 124,* 333–371.

Wheldall, K., & Limbrick, L. (2010). Do more boys than girls have reading problems? *Journal of Learning Disabilities, 43,* 418–429.

Wickenden, M. (2011). Talking to teenagers: Using anthropological methods to explore identity and the lifeworlds of young people who use AAC. *Communication Disorders Quarterly, 32,* 151–163.

Wieder, S. (1994). *Diagnostic Classification of Mental Health and Developmental Disorders of Infancy and Early Childhood. Diagnostic Classification: 0–3.* Zero to Three. Arlington, VA: /National Center for Clinical Infant Programs.

Wiggins, J. L., Mitchell, C., Hyde, L. W., & Monk, C. S. (2015). Identifying early pathways of risk and resilience: The codevelopment of internalizing and externalizing symptoms and the role of harsh parenting. *Development and Psychopathology, 27 (4pt1),* 1295–1312.

Williams, J., & Hill, P. D. (2012). *Handbook for the assessment of children's behaviours.* Chichester, UK: Wiley.

Wilson, E. O. (1975). *Sociobiology.* Cambridge, MA: Harvard University Press.

Winnicott, D. W. (1960). The theory of parent–infant relationship. *International Journal of Psycho-Analysis, 41,* 585–595.

Winnicott, D. W. (1965). Dependence towards independence. In D. W. Winnicott, *The maturational process and the facilitating environment* (pp. 83–92). London: Hogarth Press.

Witherington, D. C. (2014). Self-organization and explanatory pluralism: Avoiding the snares of reductionism in developmental science. *Research in Human Development, 11,* 22–36.

Witten, M. R. (1997). Mood disorder: Depression of infancy and early childhood. In A. Lieberman, S. Wieder & E. Fenichel (Eds), *DC: 0–3 Case book* (pp. 81–107). Washington, DC: Zero to Three.

Wolcott, H. F. (1994). *Transforming qualitative data: Description, analysis and interpretation.* Thousand Oaks, CA: Sage.

Woolley, G. (2010). A multiple strategy framework supporting vocabulary development for students with reading comprehension deficits. *Australasian Journal of Special Education, 34,* 119–132.

World Health Organization (WHO) (2001). *International classification of functioning, disability and health.* Geneve, Switzerland: World Health Organization.

World Health Organization (WHO) (2007). *International classification of functioning, disability and health: Children and youth version.* Geneve, Switzerland: World Health Organization.

World Health Organization (WHO) (2018). *The international statistical classification of diseases and related health problems, ICD-11.* Geneve, Switzerland: World Health Organization.

Wright, B. (2008). Development in deaf and blind children. *Psychiatry, 7,* 286–289.

Yiend, J., Parnes, C., Shepherd, K., Roche, M. K., & Cooper, M. J. (2014). Negative self-beliefs in eating disorders: A cognitive-bias-modification study. *Clinical Psychological Science, 2*, 756–766.

Yin, R. K. (2009). *Case study research: Design and methods*, Fourth edition. Thousand Oaks, CA: Sage.

Yoshida, H., & Smith, L. B. (2008). What's in view for toddlers? Using a head camera to study visual experience. *Infancy, 13*, 229–248.

Yoshikawa, H., Weisner, T. S., Kalil, A., & Way, N. (2008). Mixing qualitative and quantitative research in developmental science: Uses and methodological choices. *Developmental Psychology, 44*, 344–354.

Zambo, D. (2004). Using qualitative methods to understand the educational experiences of students with dyslexia. *The Qualitative Report, 9*, 80–93.

Zebehazy, K. T., Zigmond, N., & Zimmerman, G. J. (2012). Ability or accessability: Differential item functioning of items on alternate performance-based assessment tests for students with visual impairments. *Journal of Visual Impairment and Blindness, 106*, 325–338.

Zelazo, P. D. (2013). Developmental psychology: A new synthesis. In P. D. Zelazo (Ed.), *The Oxford handbook of developmental psychology*, Volume 2 (pp. 2–12). New York, NY: Oxford University Press.

Zill, N. (1996). Family change and student achievement: What we have learned, what it means for schools. In A. Booth & J. F. Dunn (Eds), *Family-school links* (pp. 139–174). Mahwah, NJ: Erlbaum.

Ziv, Y. (2013). Social information processing patterns, social skills, and school readiness in preschool children. *Journal of Experimental Child Psychology, 114*, 306–320.

Zwaigenbaum, L., Thurm, A., Stone, W., Baranek, G., Bryson, S., Iverson, J., Kau, A., Klin, A., Lord, C., Landa, R., et al. (2007). Studying the emergence of autism spectrum disorders in high-risk infants: Methodological and practical issues. *Journal of Autism and Developmental Disorders, 37*, 466–480.

Index

Note: Page Numbers in *italic* refer to Figures; Page Numbers in **bold** refer to Boxes

ABA *see* applied behavior analysis (ABA)
aberrant development 29, 30, 36
academic performance 16, 18, 109
accident injury 28, 120, 123, 147
acquired disorders 146, 149
acquired hearing loss 121
activity theory 58, 76
adaptation 26, 33, 34, 52–54, 61, 72, 137
adaptive behavior 26, 129
adaptive function 129
ADD *see* attention deficit disorder (ADD)
addiction 144–145, 149
ADHD *see* attention deficit hyperactivity disorder (ADHD)
adolescents 3, 117; addictions 144; alcohol abuse 144; antisocial behavior **20**; anxiety disorders 137; behavioral disorders 14, 26; bipolar disorder 137; bullying 86; depression 135, 136, 148; identity formation 14; Internet gaming addiction 145–146, 149; mobility impairments 101; separation anxiety 138; social anxiety disorder 138; substance abuse 144, 149
adulthood 3–4, 14, 25, 26
affective disorders 135, 148
Africa 8
aggression **20**, 76, 92

alcohol abuse 144, 149
allele **17**
altruism 60, 76
anamnestic interview 104
anger 20, 81, 134, 138
anorexia 140, 148; *see also* bulimia
antisocial behavior **20**
anxiety disorders 137–139, 148; generalized anxiety disorder 139, 148; phobias 137, 138, 148; separation anxiety 137–138, 148; social anxiety disorder 138–139, 148
applied behavior analysis (ABA) 51
applied developmental science 32
archival research 88, 94, 112
articulation disorders 125–126, 147–148
assessment 104–110, 113; checklists 105, 107–108, 113; dynamic assessment 107, 109, 110, 113; feedback 106, 110; intervention responses 109–110; interviews 104, 112; observations 105, 113; tests 105–107, 108, 109
assimilation 61
attachment 47, 76
attachment behaviors 63; Strange Situation 84
attention deficit disorder (ADD) 28, 131–132

attention deficit hyperactivity disorder (ADHD) 131–132, 147, 148
atypical development 9–10, 21–22, 23, 35
atypical language development 126
autism spectrum disorder 10, 94, 117, 130–131, 137, 147, 148
autonomy 4

Batten disease see juvenile neuronal ceroid lipofuscinosis, JNCLbehavioral disorders 3, 14, 26, 118–119, 133–140, 148
behavioral shaping 48
behaviorism 39, 47–51, 73, 75
behavior observation see observations
behavior therapy 51
bio-ecological theory 64–67, 76; exosystem 65, 66, 76; macrosystem 65, 67, 76; mesosystem 65, 66, 67, 76; microsystem 65, 67, 76
biological factors 12
bipolar disorder 136–137, 148
blindness 10, 22, 120–121
brain damage 120, 147, 148
bulimia 140, 148; see also anorexia
bullying 41, 86, 103

cascade 26–27, 36
case study 91–92, 113
CBCL see Child Behavior Check List
cerebral palsy 123, 147
checklist 105, 107–108, 113
Child Behavior Check List (CBCL) 108
child-directed speech 94
childhood psychology 70, 77
children: anxiety disorders 137; behavioral disorders 26; bipolar disorder 137; bullying 86; consent 111; depression 135; generalized anxiety disorder 139; Internet gaming addiction 149; separation anxiety 137–138; social anxiety disorder 138–139

children at play (at home with parents) **83**
China 7
classical conditioning 47, 97; see also conditioning
classification systems, international 118–119
cleft spine see spina bifida (cleft spine)
clinical assessment see assessment
clinical method (Piaget) 101
clinical psychology 46, 51, 92, 113
clinical study 91, 92; see also case study
Cognitive behavior theory 50, 51
cognitive conflict 53–54, 72
cognitive development 12, 25–26, 41, 45–46, 52–59, 72–73
cognitive learning theory 75
cognitive structures 26, 47, 53–54
cognitive tests 110
combined visual and hearing impairment 147
communication disorders 147
comorbidity 125, 140
concept learning 23–24
conditioning: classical 47, 97; infants 96, 97, 113; operant 47, 97
conduct disorder 134–135
conduct-dissocial disorder 134
conductive hearing loss 121
consent 111, 114
constructivism 52; logical 39, 52–55, 75–76; social 39, 56–59, 76, 109
construct validity 102, 103
continuity 12
control group 91, 103, 112–113
core knowledge 60
cortical visual impairment 120; see also blindness
critical developmental psychology 39, 70, 77
critical period 13
cross-cultural study 7, 35, 94–95, 113
cross-sectional study 92, 93, 113
cultural differences 11
cultural tools 56, 58, 72, 76
culture 72

DC 0–3: Diagnostic Classification of Mental Health and Developmental Disorders of Infancy and Early Childhood 118, 147; anxiety disorders 137; mood disorders 135; post-traumatic stress disorder 142
deaf 9, 121
deafblindness 122
deconstruction 70
defense mechanisms 45, 75
depression 135–136, 148
developmental coordination disorder 124
developmental effect 15
developmental model 24–25
developmental motor coordination disorder (dyspraxia) 107, 124, 147
developmental pathway 23, 34
developmental phase 26, 58, 64
developmental psychopathology 33–34, 36
developmental risk 28–31
developmental science 6, 14, 15
developmental stage 12–13
developmental way of thinking 31–32, 36, 73–74
deviant development 13, 14, 45
Diagnostic and Statistical Manual of Mental Disorders (DSM-5) 118, 119, 147
diagnostic shadowing 146
diagnostic systems 117; *see also* assessment
diary study 82
diathesis–stress model 30, 36
differential continuity 12
difficult temperament 16
discontinuity 12
disequilibrium 53–54
dishabituation 96, 113
disinhibited social engagement disorder 141–142, 148–149
disruptive behaviors 133
disruptive mood dysregulation disorder 136
distress 72, 138, 141, 142

dissocial disorder 133
drive 42–44, 48
drives-theory 42–44
DSM-5 *see Diagnostic and Statistical Manual of Mental Disorders* (DSM-5)
Duchenne muscular dystrophy 123
dynamic assessment 107, 109, 110, 113
dynamic model 26
dynamic system 23–25, 26, 35–6
dyscalculia (mathematics disorders) 128, 148
dyslexia (reading and writing disorders) 103, 127–128, 148; *see also* learning disorders
dyspraxia (developmental coordination disorder) 107, 124, 147; *see also* learning disorders
dysthymic disorder 135

easy temperament 18
eating disorders 140, 148; anorexia 140, 148; bulimia 140, 148
ecological psychology 39, 64–67
ecological stage 49
ecological system 65–66
ego 43, 44, 75
ego psychology 45
emotional disorder 3, 133
emotional expression 95
emotional regulation 95
emotion regulation disorder 134
empathy 34
enculturation 4, 57
epilepsy 128, 146
equifinality 13
equilibrium 53–54
ethical committee 114
ethics 111, 113–114
ethological psychology 39, 63, 73
ethological theory 63, 76
evolution 60, 61–62
evolutionary psychology 39, 60–62, 70, 76
exosystem 65, 66, 76

experimental group 91, 112
experiments 83–85, 90, 112; field
    experiments 84–85, 112; laboratory
    experiments 84, 112
exploration 9–10; visual 96, 97, 113
externalizing disorder 133, 148
external validity 103
extroverted children 18

family income 16, 18
fear-related disorders *see* anxiety
    disorders; phobias
field experiments 84–85, 112
fluency disorders 126
fragile X syndrome 19
frustration 26, 136

gambling disorder 145
gaming disorder 144–145, 149
gender roles 71
generalized anxiety disorder 139, 148
gene 15–16, 47, 60, 61, 76
genetic disorders 11, 15
globalization 7, 8, 35
grammatical impairments 126
gross motor skills 103
group study 90–91, 112–113

habituation 96, 113
hard of hearing 121
hearing impairment 9, 28, 120, 121,
    126, 147
heredity 11
heterotypic continuity 12
homotypic continuity 12
Horowitz's model 30
Huntington's disease 15
hyperactivity 131
hyperlexia 128

ICD-11 *see International Statistical
    Classification of Diseases and Related
    Health Problems* (ICD-11)
ICF *see International Classification of
    Functioning, Disability and Health* (ICF)
ICF-CY *see International Classification
    of Functioning, Disability and Health,
    Children and Youth Version* (ICF-CY)

id 43, 44, 75
identity formation 14
imbalance 36
imitation 47
immigrant children 105–106
imprinting 63
impulse control 134
impulsivity 131, 136, 148
India 7–8
individual child studies 91–92, 113
individual differences 4, 11
individuation 44
infants 96–99, 113; cognition
    99; conditioning 96, 97, 113;
    dishabituation 96, 113; habituation
    96, 113; neurophysiological
    measures 98, 113; physiological
    response 98, 113; preferential
    looking 97–98, 113; visual
    exploration 96, 97, 113
information collection: archival data
    88; interview 86–87, 90, 104, 112;
    observation 73, 81–85, 90, 112;
    questionnaires 86, 90, 112
information processing 39, 68–69,
    76–77
inner psychic structures 42, 75
intellectual disabilities 9, 127,
    129–130, 147, 148; intelligence
    129
intelligence test 102, 110, 129
interaction developmental model
    29–30
interaction effects 15, 16–18, 35; main
    effects 15–16, 18, 35; maternal
    sensitivity **17**; transaction effects 15,
    18–22, 35
intermittent explosive disorder
    134
internalization 56, 58, 72, 76
internalizing disorders 133, 148
internal validity 103
*International Classification of Functioning,
    Disability and Health, Children and
    Youth Version* (ICF-CY) 118–119,
    147
*International Classification of Functioning,
    Disability and Health* (ICF) 118, 119

International Statistical Classification of Diseases and Related Health Problems (ICD-11) 118, 119, 147
Internet addiction 145, 149
Internet gaming addiction 144–145, 149
inter-observer reliability 101–102
interview 86–87, 90, 104, 112
IQ *see* intelligence; intelligence test

joint attention 47
juvenile neuronal ceroid lipofuscinosis (JNCL, Batten disease) 120–121

kindergarten 21, 28, 88, 90, 105, 108, 137

laboratory experiment 84, 112
Landau-Kleffner syndrome 146
language development 10, 13, 28, 61, 94, 126, 147
language disorders 125–126, 127–128, 147–148
language instinct 60
learning disorders 3, 127, 147
learning mechanisms 47
Learning Potential Assessment Device 109
libido 43, 44
life space 64
linear developmental model 24
logical constructivism 39, 52–55, 75–76
longitudinal study 92–93, 113

macrosystem 65, 67, 76
main effect 15–16, 18, 35
maternal depression **20**
maternal sensitivity **17**, 19
mathematics disorders (dyscalculia) 128, 148
M-CHAT 108
Mean Length of utterance (MLU) 89
mental disorders 36, 42, 118–119, 148
mental model 60–61
mesosystem 65, 66, 67, 76
microgenetic study 90, 112
microsystem 65, 67, 76

mind understanding 10
mismatch response 98
mixed methods 90, 112
mobility 9–10
mobility impairment 9–10, 22, 101
module 60, 61
mood disorders 135, 148
moral development 4, 12, 73, 76
motivating operation 48
motor impairments 107, 123–124, 147; cerebral palsy 123, 147; developmental coordination disorder 124; spina bifida 123, 124, 147
multicultural environment 4
multifinality 13–14

nativism 60–62, 76
naturalistic observations 82, 112
nature versus nurture 7, 16
neo-Piagetians 54–55, 76
neo-Vygotskians 58, 76
neurodevelopmental disorders 124, 125–132, 147; attention deficit hyperactivity disorder 131–132, 147, 148; autism spectrum disorder 10, 94, 117, 130–131, 137, 147, 148; intellectual disabilities 9, 127, 129–130, 147, 148; language disorders 125–126, 127–128, 147–148; learning disorders 3, 127, 147; mathematics disorders 128, 148; reading and writing disorder 103, 127–128, 148
neurogenic hearing loss 121
neurophysiological measure 98, 113
new theory (Piaget) 55, 76
non-compliance and infant aggression **20**
non-linear developmental model 24–25
non-representative sample 103
nonverbal task 107
Noonan syndrome 18
Normal distribution 129
norm-referenced test 107
norms 105–107, 108, 109, 113
novelty preference 97–98

obedience 19
object permanence 54
object relations theory 44, 75
observation 73, 81–85, 90, 112;
    assessment 105, 113; checklist 105,
    107–108, 113; children at play
    83; experiment 83–85; reliability
    101–102; test 113
obsessive-compulsive disorder (OCD)
    139–140, 148
operant (instrumental) conditioning
    47, 97
oppositional defiant disorder 132, 134
orienting response 98

paediatric bipolar disorder 136
parenting 18–21, **83**, **88**, 95, 111, 114
perceptual problems 120
persistent depressive disorder 135
personality 42, 44, 61, 72, 73
personality trait 45
phobia 137, 138, 148
phonological disorders 126, 128
physiological response 98, 113
play 3, 81, 82, **83**, 94, 105, 139, 145
pleasure principle 43
population sample 101, 113
positive development 28–29, 30, 31,
    36
post-traumatic stress disorder (PTSD)
    142–143, 149
pragmatic disorders 126
predictive validity 102
preferential looking (visual preference)
    99; infants 97–98, 113
prelingual hearing loss 121
preparedness 19
prevention 34
progressive disorders 146
prolonged grief reaction 135
prospective studies 93, 94, 113; *see also*
    retrospective studies
proximal processes 64, 76
psychoanalytic theory: ego 43, 44,
    75; id 43, 44, 75; libido 43, 44;
    psychosexual phases 45; reality
    principle 43; superego 43, 44, 75;
    thanatos 43

psychodynamic psychology 39, 42–46,
    73, 75
psychopathology 34
psychosexual phases 45

qualitative change 4
qualitative difference 4
qualitative research method
    89–90, 101, 112; reliability 102;
    transparency 100–101; validity 103
quantifiable difference 4
quantitative research method 89, 90,
    112
questionnaire 86, 90, 112

reactive attachment disorder 141,
    148–149
reading and writing disorders
    (dyslexia) 103, 127–128, 148
reality construction 56
reality principle 43
redefinition 21–22
re-education 21, 22
relational psychoanalysis 46
reliability 101–102, 113
remediation 21
replicability 100
representative sample 101, 113
research methods 100, 112–113
resilience 28–29, 30, 36
respondent (classical) conditioning *see*
    classical conditioning
response to intervention 109–110
responsiveness 141
retrospective study 93–94, 113
Rett syndrome 15, 30
risk 28–31, 36
Rosenthal effect 84–85

selective mutism 139, 148
self 45, 75
self-efficacy 73
self-image 45, 73
self-propelled mobility 13
self-regulation 23–24
semantic impairments 126
sensitive periods 13
sensitivity to consequences 48

sensory impairments 120–122, 147; blindness 10, 22, 120–121; deafblindness 122; hearing impairments 9, 28, 120, 121, 126, 147; visual impairments 9, 120–121, 147
separation 44
separation anxiety 137–138, 148
shy 3, 18, 69, 73, 85, 90–91, 139
sign language 9, 126
snowball effect 27
social adaptation 26
social affiliation 4
social anxiety disorder 138–139, 148
social class 7–8, 88, 101
social constructivism 39, 56–59, 76, 109
social crises theory 45
social learning theory 50, 51
social media 144–145, 149
social referencing 47
social relationships 4
societal development 7
societal stage 49
socioeconomic status (SES) **88**
specific language impairment (SLI) 126
spina bifida (cleft spine) 123, 124, 147
spinal muscular atrophy 123
stability 12
stage theory 13
standard theory *see* new theory (Piaget)
static system 23
statistics 89
Strange Situation 84
stress 98
stressor-related disorders 141–143, 148–149
stuttering 126
substance abuse 144, 149
suicide 145
superego 43, 44, 75
survival 41, 48, 60, 63, 76

survival drive 48
symbolic 45, 46

temperament 12, 16, 18, 61
temper tantrums 12
tests 105–107, 108, 109, 113
test–training–test procedure 110
thanatos 43
theory of mind *see* mind understanding
toddlers 135, 137
Tourette syndrome 140
training–test–training procedure 110
traits 9, 11, 14, 15–16, 28
transactional chain 18–21
transaction effect 15, 18–22, 35
transaction model 18–22
transformation 3
transparency 100–101, 113
trauma-related disorders 141–143, 148–149
tripartite consciousness 45–46

unconscious motive 44–45, 75
universal stage 49
unreliability 101–102
Usher syndrome 122

validity 102–103, 113
Vineland Adaptive Behavior Scale 108
violence 62, 142
visual exploration 96, 97, 113
visual impairments 9, 120–121, 147
visual perception 128
visual preference *see* preferential looking (visual preference)
voice difficulties 126
vulnerability 3, 28–31, 33–34, 36

walking 25
war 30, 127, 142

zone of proximal development 57, 109

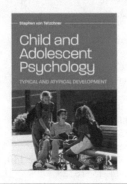

The **Topics from Child and Adolescent Psychology Series** is drawn from Stephen von Tetzchner's comprehensive textbook for all students of developmental psychology, *Child and Adolescent Psychology: Typical and Atypical Development*

Table of Contents

1: Developmental Psychology 2: Theoretical Perspectives 3: Methods of Gaining Knowledge about Children 4: Child and Adolescent Disorders 5: Genes, Evolution, Heredity and Environment 6: Stimulation and Activity During Fetal Development 7: Brain Development 8: Perceptual Development 9: Motor Development 10: Theories of Cognitive Development 11: Attention, Memory and Executive Function 12: Conceptual Development and Reasoning 13: Mind Understanding 14: Intelligence 15: Learning and Instruction 16: The Development of Communication and Language 17: Emotions and Emotion Regulation 18: Temperament and Personality 19: Attachment 20: Sibling and Peer Relations 21: Self and Identity 22: Moral Development 23 Prosocial and Antisocial Development 24: Gender Development 25: Play 26: Media and Understanding of Society 27: Toward Adulthood

Praise for *Child and Adolescent Psychology: Typical and Atypical Development*

'An extensive overview of the field of developmental psychology. It illustrates how knowledge about typical and atypical development can be integrated and used to highlight fundamental processes of human growth and maturation.'

Dr. John Coleman, *PhD, OBE, UK*

'A broad panoply of understandings of development from a wide diversity of perspectives and disciplines, spanning all the key areas, and forming a comprehensive, detailed and extremely useful text for students and practitioners alike.'

Dr. Graham Music, *Consultant Psychotherapist, Tavistock Clinic London, UK*

'An extraordinary blend of depth of scholarship with a lucid, and engaging, writing style. Its coverage is impressive . . . Both new and advanced students will love the coverage of this text.'

Professor Joseph Campos, *University of California, USA*

'Encyclopedic breadth combined with an unerring eye for the central research across developmental psychology, particularly for the period of its explosive growth since the 1960s. Both a text and a reference work, this will be the go-to resource for any teacher, researcher or student of the discipline for the foreseeable future.'

Professor Andy Lock, *University of Lisbon, Portugal*

It is accompanied by a companion website featuring chapter summaries, glossary, quizzes and instructor resources.